Giovanni Maria Cornoldi, Edward Heneage Dering

The Physical System Of St. Thomas

Giovanni Maria Cornoldi, Edward Heneage Dering

The Physical System Of St. Thomas

ISBN/EAN: 9783743462809

Manufactured in Europe, USA, Canada, Australia, Japa

Cover: Foto ©Suzi / pixelio.de

Manufactured and distributed by brebook publishing software (www.brebook.com)

Giovanni Maria Cornoldi, Edward Heneage Dering

The Physical System Of St. Thomas

THE PHYSICAL SYSTEM
OF ST. THOMAS.

BY THE SAME AUTHOR.

Principles of Political Economy. By MATTEO LIBERATORE, S.J. Translated by EDWARD HENEAGE DERING, author of "Freville Chase," etc. 8vo, cloth, bevelled, 7s. 6d.

On Universals. An Exposition of Thomistic Doctrine. By MATTEO LIBERATORE, S.J. Translated by E. H. DERING. In wrapper, 7s. 6d. Bound in vellum, 10s. 6d.

The Atherstone Novels, by E. H. DERING.

The Lady of Raven's Combe. 2 vols., 7s. 6d. ; in one vol., 5s.

Freville Chase. *New Edition.* 2 vols., 7s. 6d. : in one vol., 5s.

The Ban of Maplethorpe. *In the Press.*

Sherborne ; or, The House at the Four Ways. *New Edition. To follow.*

THE
PHYSICAL SYSTEM
OF ST. THOMAS

BY

FATHER GIOVANNI MARIA CORNOLDI, S.J.

TRANSLATED BY

EDWARD HENEAGE DERING

*Translator of "On Universals," and "Political Economy;"
Author of "Freville Chase," "The Ban of Maplethorpe," "Memoirs
of Georgiana Lady Chatterton," &c., &c.*

LONDON AND LEAMINGTON
Art and Book Company
NEW YORK, CINCINNATI & CHICAGO: BENZIGER BROS.
1893

BEFORE the last chapter of this treatise was in print, its lamented author had passed out of this world, in which he had done invaluable service to the Church of GOD.

While the present translation was passing through the press, the translator also, EDWARD HENEAGE DERING, was suddenly called to his reward. The last composition that he printed (in the *Tablet*, Nov. 19, 1892), was the following short memoir of his friend and master in Scholastic science, FATHER MATTEO LIBERATORE:

"In Memoriam.

"Sixty-seven years ago a boy of fifteen, whose book-learning had till then been in abeyance, by reason of his having wonderfully been the mainstay of his widowed mother's house from the age of ten, entered a Jesuit school in Naples, and, rapidly passing all his competitors, was in the following year a novice in the Society of JESUS. He was Professor of Philosophy from 1837—only twelve years after going to school—till the Revolution of 1848 forced him into exile, from which he returned at the imminent risk of his life, and was made Professor of Theology at Naples. The risk was evident, because his name was on the list of the proscribed, as intended for the patriot's dagger. In 1850 he co-operated in founding the *Civiltà Cattolica*, to defend the Church, the Holy See, and notably the teaching of ST. THOMAS. Without him that invaluable periodical would have died still-born, instead of doing the great work that it has done and continues to do. But this necessitates a brief retrospect. When he began teaching philosophy as a professor, thirteen years before, he found it infected with dangerous errors. We cannot speak of them here for want of space, but certain it is that the Angelic Doctor was generally forgotten, discredited, misrepresented, and that false philosophy was taught even within the Church. He was the first in the field against that, published his *Institutiones Philosophicæ* in 1840, and continued to fight the good fight as long as Almighty God willed that his life should last. That man was FATHER MATTEO LIBERATORE, who died in Rome on the 18th of last October, eight months after the death of his great co-operator and *confrère*, FATHER GIOVANNI MARIA CORNOLDI. When two such men are taken away from the Church militant, one can only turn to Almighty God and say, *Fiat voluntas Tua*. To myself the loss of FATHER LIBERATORE is a personal grief and an irreparable loss. *Dominus dedit. . . Dominus abstulit. . . sit nomen Domini benedictum.—Baddesley Clinton*, Nov. 19, 1892."

Mr. Dering's life and literary labours had been devoted to the enlightenment and conversion of his countrymen. He died, as he had desired to do, in harness; and, lamenting the greatness of his loss, the many who loved him, can only echo his last printed words: *Dominus dedit. . . . Dominus abstulit. . . . sit nomen Domini benedictum.*

PREFACE.

WHY THIS TREATISE WAS WRITTEN.

HAVING for many years openly defended the Philosophy of St. Thomas, even in what concerns the fundamental doctrines of organic and inorganic nature, we think it time to treat that subject, not merely touching on one or another point, but dealing with those doctrines philosophically.

In Italy, where Masonic influence is now felt in every department of Government, nothing has been omitted by which the minds and hearts of our young men could be turned away, not only from the religious teaching of the Catholic Church, but also from all philosophical doctrines that are not against Religion. The teaching of Metaphysics was made over years ago to professors who only corrupted their pupils by the German transcendentalism of Kant, Hegel, Schelling and others : but, inasmuch as that philosophy was abstruse, ill-suited to the wicked purpose intended and very apt to produce weariness, Metaphysics, properly so-called, were afterwards proscribed in the schools, to make way for Positivism and Materialism.

If in our Catholic schools Physical Sciences were rightly and fully taught, the evil would be less. But what we call Government schools are, for the most part, obligatory; and, by reason of the method prescribed, even for private schools it is impossible to elucidate those doctrines without which the pupils are neither instructed sufficiently nor prepared for resisting the temptations of the Universities.

By this treatise we cannot hope to be of use directly and immediately in the public schools of the Government: but we can hope to do something indirectly and mediately.

In the second place, many who have a great reverence for the wisdom of the Angelic Doctor, and, in obedience to the Vicar of Jesus Christ, declare their adhesion to his doctrines, know too little of the fundamental questions that belong to Physics. Many have confused ideas about them, and therefore are liable to be taken in by the sophisms and the authority of men who pass as wise and learned in such things. Hence they either give in or vacillate, accepting as probable what is not only improbable, but also absurd and bad.

These and other reasons have induced us to put before our readers, especially those who are given to the study of philosophy and natural sciences, that system which we call the Physical System, whose principles were certainly professed by the Angelic Doctor, St. Thomas. It is, or should be, unnecessary to say that we are not going to rake up exploded doctrines of the old physicists. The habit of confusing such opinions with the philosophical principles of rational Physics, ascribing to the latter what belongs to pure experiment, has led many to attack truth with the hatred due to error and to put the wisest in the category of quacks.

CONTENTS.

Chap.		Page
I.	THE ESSENCE AND NATURE OF CORPOREAL SUBSTANCES	1
II.	MATERIA PRIMA	4
III.	SUBSTANTIAL FORM	12
IV.	NATURE	21
V.	CREATION	28
VI.	ATOMS	37
VII.	SEMINAL CAUSES	46
VIII.	QUALITIES	56
IX.	ATTRACTION	69
X.	PHYSICAL LAWS	81
XI.	WHY THE PHYSICAL SYSTEM IS SO CALLED	90
XII.	THE PHYSICAL SYSTEM WITH RESPECT TO PHYSICS IN GENERAL. THE NATURE OF THIS SCIENCE	95
XIII.	MECHANICAL INERTIA AND PHYSICAL ACTIVITY OF BODIES	100
XIV.	OBJECTIONS AGAINST THE DOCTRINE PROPOSED	108

	CONTENTS.	
XV.	ACTION AT AN ABSOLUTE DISTANCE	117
XVI.	MOTION	125
XVII.	THE PRINCIPLE, "QUOD MOVETUR AB ALIO MOVETUR, ET PRIMUM MOVENS EST IMMOBILE"	138
XVIII.	THE MUTABILITY OF EXTENSION	150
XIX.	WHY THE PHYSICAL SYSTEM IS SUPPOSED TO BE IN OPPOSITION TO PHYSICS	160
XX.	ON THE DIVISIBILITY OF THE CONTINUOUS EXTENDED	163
XXI.	ETHER	170
XXII.	CHEMISTRY	177
XXIII.	ELEMENTARY ATOMS	180
XXIV.	THE MATTER AND FORM OF ELEMENTARY SUBSTANCES ARE REALLY DISTINCT	184
XXV.	AN ELEMENTARY SUBSTANCE IS CHEMICALLY SIMPLE	188
XXVI.	THE "MIXTUM," OR THE CHEMICAL COMPOUND. AFFINITY BETWEEN THE ELEMENTS	193
XXVII.	THE "MIXTUM," OR CHEMICAL COMPOUND, HAS A NATURE SPECIFICALLY DIFFERENT FROM THAT OF ITS COMPONENTS	198
XXVIII.	WHAT IS MEANT BY SUBSTANTIAL TRANSFORMATION	201

XXIX. THE COMMON SENSE OF MANKIND IS IN FAVOUR OF A BELIEF IN THE TRUE SUBSTANTIAL TRANSFORMATION OF THE ELEMENTS - - - 204

XXX. THE SUBSTANTIAL TRANSFORMATION OF THE ELEMENTS IS PROVED BY FACTS - - - 207

XXXI. OPPOSITION TO THE DOCTRINE OF SUBSTANTIAL TRANSFORMATION - - - - - - 211

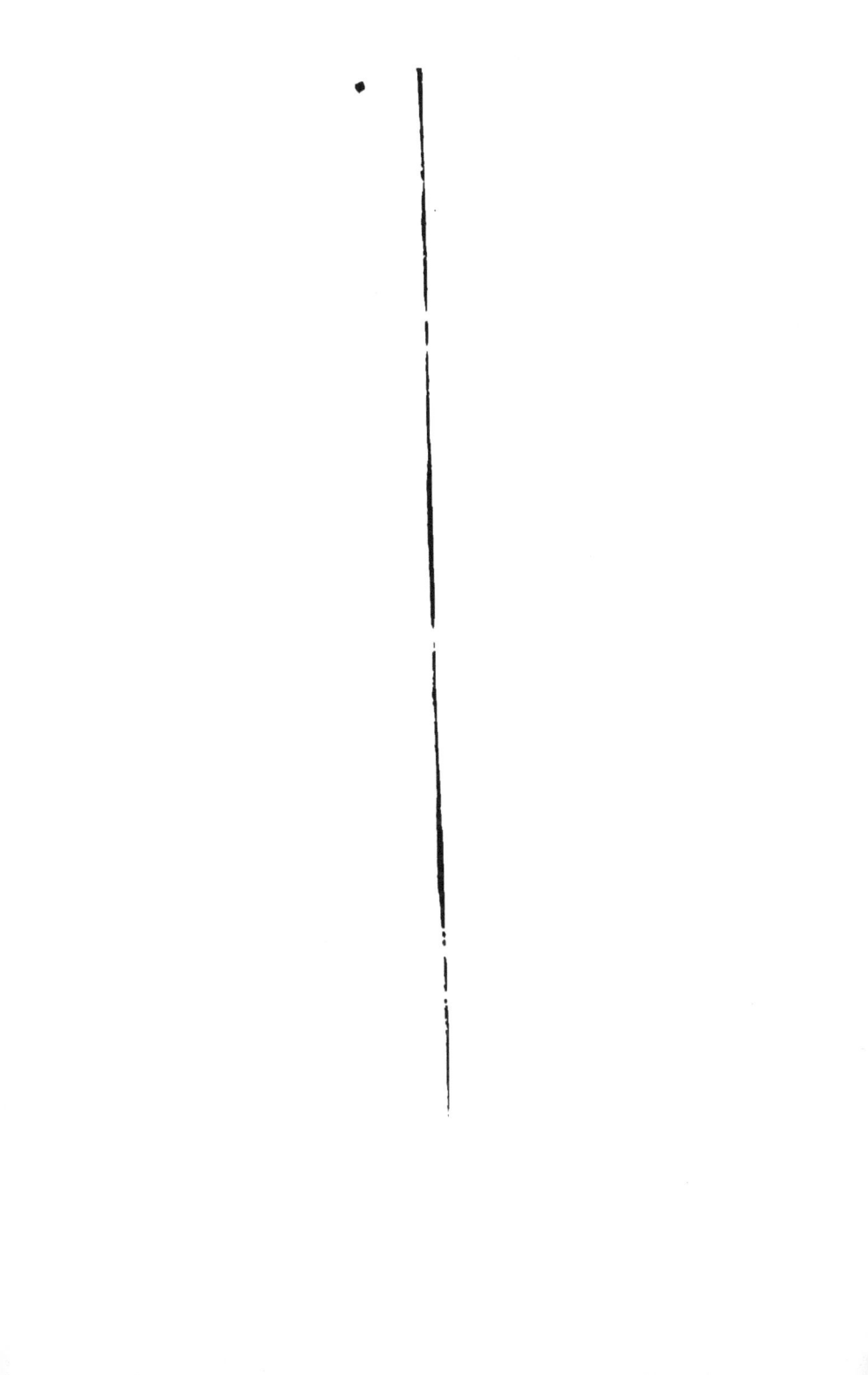

THE PHYSICAL SYSTEM OF ST. THOMAS.

I

THE ESSENCE AND NATURE OF CORPOREAL SUBSTANCES.

THERE is nothing perhaps harder to defend and easier to attack than a system not clearly defined, at least in its principal parts. Its defenders waste their time in showing what is either beside the question or only touches the surface, and its adversaries, when they have pointed out the weak points in that which, true or false, has nothing to do with the truth of the system, settle the controversy in their own favour.

To avoid this, we shall explain without delay the system of which we are going to treat; and, first of all, we must remark that it differs from the Mechanic and Dynamic systems as to the very essence of corporeal substances. According to the Mechanic system, corporeal substance means inert and resisting atoms aggregated in varying order. The Dynamic system recognizes subsisting forces only, as in mathematical points of space. The Physical system supposes that every individual corporeal substance is essentially composed of two principles really distinct. One is the source of extension, and is called *materia prima*. The other is the source of activity, and is called the *substantial form*. On the variety of the latter the diversities of nature in every substance depend. The *materia prima* and the substantial form, being incomplete substances, cannot be apart. God did not create matter quite without form, but endowed it with diverse forms actuated with virtues that may be called seminal, radically containing the whole order and beauty of the sensible universe, which by degrees developed and in the course of time is continually developing. During this continual development we perceive changes in substances, in their qualities and in their accidents, and in their mutual approach and departure. In the former case there is a true change of substantial forms, the matter of one body being transmuted into that of another. In the second there is a change of accidental forms only. In the third, unless there is some mechanical impulse, one body is brought towards another by true attraction. From such forms and such properties, impressed on creation, a determinate development of the corporeal universe necessarily follows; and in these forms and in these properties we must recognize the existence of physical laws, considered, not as in the Mind or Will of the Creator, but as an effect in the created things themselves.

But this is too rapid a sketch. We must consider each part of the system in detail.

II.

MATERIA PRIMA.

THE very ancient philosophers, the beginners in philosophy, held that corporeal substances are nothing more than aggregations of atoms, either inert, or, at the most, endowed with attractive and repulsive force, like some sort of sympathy and antipathy. Afterwards Plato taught the doctrine of Matter and Form, infected however with grave errors, which Aristotle partly corrected, and which the Catholic Doctors, the only philosophers who had a clear and firm conception of God the Creator, afterwards rooted out. "The ancient philosophers," says St. Thomas, "came to the knowledge of truth slowly and by degrees. For at first, as being less cultivated, they recognized no other beings than sensible bodies; and those among them who acknowledged movement in such, admitted that sort of movement only which takes place in some accidents, as in rarity and density, by aggregation and disgregation. Afterwards, supposing corporeal substance to be uncreated, they assigned some causes for their accidental changes, as, for instance, friendship, strife and such like. Thence they went on to distinguish substantial form and matter, which they supposed to be uncreated, and they perceived that substantial transmutations happen in bodies."*

We shall proceed to enquire how they came to this knowledge.

Plato in his *Timæus* remarks that in the sensible universe every being is subject to substantial changes without a continual annihilation of previous things and continual creation of succeeding ones. Hence he inferred that in this changing of substance there always remains a substratum, or subject,—a matter which is adapted and transformed successively into various natures. Thus fluids become plants, and plants become the flesh of brutes and even of man. And, since by such transforming of matter the eternal forms or ideas are determined, there must be in the universe a matter that is itself deprived of all determinate nature and is disposed for receiving those species which it derives from the communication or impression of the archetypal ideas. "Three things," he says, "have here to be distinguished: that which is generated (the new nature); that in which it is generated (the matter); that from which the generated thing gets its proper likeness (the idea or form). Now, if these things

---

* *Summa*, P. i. Q. xliv. a. 2.

be compared, the nature generated resembles an offspring; the thing in which it is generated resembles a mother; and that from which it gets its likeness resembles a father. This doctrine must be understood to mean that, as the forms of things are distinguished by every sort of variety, this womb [i.e. matter, thereto compared] could never be well disposed for the formations to be produced in it, unless it were formless, quite void of all forms whatsoever; because, if it already had in itself any of those natures for which it is in a state of potentiality, it would not be capable of receiving a contrary form. Thus, if it were essentially water, how could it be changed into wood? It would inconceivably be at once water and wood. But, as it is potentially all these things, it cannot have the form of any, just as modelling clay has none. As the matter of scented unguents is purposely without scent, and modelling clay has no shape till the artist has modelled it, so the thing that is to be modelled according to the eternal ideas must have no form natural to itself. Therefore the mother, or receptacle of the corporeal universe, is neither earth, nor air, nor fire, nor water, nor that which constitutes their nature, nor something else composed of them, but rather it is a certain invisible something, a formless womb, potentially everything, incomprehensibly participating in the Divine nature through the impression that it receives from the archetypal ideas. Such a womb cannot be known as it is, but only as we have explained it." In these words Plato gives us a doctrine almost perfect as to the essence of bodies; but he spoilt it by his theory of ideas subsisting outside the Divine Mind, and by his belief that the matter which receives the impression of them is eternal.

St. Augustine, who was a great admirer of Plato, vainly sought from learned men that knowledge of matter which he afterwards gained when he had considered the passing of things from one substantial form to another, and seen that all through the change between two terms there must remain in both something identical and itself indifferent to both. "O my God," he said, "if I were to speak or write what Thou hast taught me about this! When I heard of it from those who understood it not, I heard the name without knowing what it meant, and, thinking of it under innumerable forms, precisely for that reason thought not of it as it is. Ugly and horrible forms passed in disorder through my mind; but forms they were all the while. I called them formless, not as being without form, but because they were such that the sight of them was too strange and hideous for human infirmity to bear. That of which I thought was not formless by privation of all form, but only in comparison with more beautiful forms; and right reason showed me that, if I wanted to think of the formless, I must take quite away all remains whatsoever of form. But this I was unable to do; for I could think more easily that what has no form is nothing, than think of something between a thing formed of nothing, not formed and not nothing, formless and therefore near to nothing. Then, instead of continuing to imagine various changes of bodies already formed, I fixed my attention on the bodies themselves, examining more deeply their mutability, how they cease to be what they were, and begin to be what they were not; and I suspected that such passing on from form to form must be through a something without form, yet not pure nothing. But I wanted to know, not to conjecture. If I could unfold all that in this question Thou hast made clear, who among my readers would be able to understand it? But my heart will never cease to give thanks and praise for what it cannot express." *

That St. Thomas formed his conception of *materia prima* in the same way is evident in many passages. Here is one of them: "He

---

* *Confess.*, l. xii. c. 6.

[Aristotle] declares the aforesaid principles, and affirms that the nature firstly subject to change, i.e. *materia prima*, cannot itself be known, inasmuch as things are known through their form, while *materia prima* is the subject of every form. The thing is known by analogy, i.e. according to proportion. Thus we know that wood is something really distinct from the form of a bench or of a bed, because the wood is sometimes under the one form and sometimes under the other. When therefore we see that what was air becomes water, we must say that there is something existing beneath the forms of natural substances," (for instance, under the form of water and the form of air,) "just as in artificial ones, wood is something besides the form of a bench or the form of a bed, or copper is something besides the form of a statue. Therefore that which is to natural substances as copper is to a statue and wood is to bed, and every material and formless thing is to its form, that thing we call *materia prima*."*

Materia prima is then the SUBJECT OF ALL THE SUBSTANTIAL TRANSFORMATIONS OF THE CORPOREAL UNIVERSE, which from the beginning of the world, while the various natures of things have perished and are perishing to make way for new ones, has remained and remains always the same. Yet some people believe that St.

---
* *In I. Phys.*, lect. xiii.

Thomas understood *materia prima* to mean pure nothing or the possibility of forms; and this in defiance of such passages, for instance, as the following in the *Summa Theologica*, P. i. Q. xiv. a. xi. ad 3, where we read :— *Materia, licet recedat a Dei similitudine secundum suam potentialitatem, tamen, in quantum vel sic esse habet, similitudinem quamdam retinet divini esse.* And in the *Quæstiones Disputatæ, De Verit.* Q. iii. a. v. ad 1, he says: *Quamvis materia prima sit informis, tamen inest in ea imitatio primæ formæ. Quantumcumque debile esse habeat, illud tamen est imitatio primi entis; et secundum hoc potest habere similitudinem in Deo.*

The followers of the Mechanic and Dynamic systems have quite a different conception of *materia prima*. The former suppose it to be inert atoms, while the latter consider it as a subsisting form in the manner of mathematical points. According to these two theories the atoms and the forces would not be the *subject* of substance, but true substances. An atom of oxygen, for instance, which with hydrogen forms water, is not merely an atom, but has the nature of oxygen, not that of hydrogen; whereas, according to the doctrine of Plato, Aristotle, St. Augustine, St. Thomas, and so many other men of noble genius who followed them, the potential entity which was there constituted in the nature of oxygen, and which afterwards, by union with hydrogen, became water, is *materia prima*. It is called *prima* to mark it as the first requisite for bodies, in order to constitute their substantial being, which substantial being is first; and also to distinguish it from that which is called *materia secunda* (secondary matter), which becomes the subject of various accidental modifications. We must now speak of the form whence that primary constitution proceeds.

III.

SUBSTANTIAL FORM.

IN Latin the word *forma* was used to signify *idea*, and was applied to the exemplar of a work, whether it be in the mind of the artist or expressed materially.

Nec vero, says Cicero, *ille artifex, cum faceret Jovis formam aut Minervæ, contemplabatur aliquem a quo similitudinem duceret, sed ipsius in mente insidebat species, quam contuens in eaque defixus, ad illius similitudinem artem et manum dirigebat....Has rerum formas appellabat ideas ille, non intelligendi solum, sed etiam dicendi, gravissimus auctor et magister Plato, easque gigni negat, et ait semper esse, a ratione et intelligentia contineri; cetera nasci, occidere, fluere, labi, nec diutius esse uno et eodem statu.*

The substantial form of anything is, philosophically speaking, THE LIKENESS OF A DIVINE IDEA, WHICH BEING EXPRESSED IN MATTER CONSTITUTES IT IN A DETERMINATE SUBSTANCE; as, for example, the entity whence the matter of gold is constituted in its proper substantial being.

From the variety of these forms results the distinction of Genera and Species. These, adorning the sensible universe, present beautiful images of those exemplars which are in the Divine Mind. Hence Plato and Aristotle with their followers gave to those forms names that indicate order and beauty, even calling them a divine thing, a participation of GOD, the *one* from which every substance receives unity. And Albert the Great approves of these, adding more of his own, especially where he takes into consideration the names adapted to signify form in its twofold relations, viz. as the term of the artist's action expressed in matter, and as that which constitutes the matter in a determinate being. "The names of form," he says, "are various, inasmuch as it is the end of motion, and constitutes in being the thing formed. In the former sense it is said to be something divine, something most excellent, something desirable.... In the latter sense it is called *form*, as giving form and as distinguishing formless matter; and *species*, as constituting the thing in its being, thus rendering it knowable; *reason*, as having in it the definition of the thing; *idea, paradigma, image*, as proceeding from its exemplar, which is in the First Cause, because every form impressed in matter was at first in the First Mover, called by Plato the archetypal world, according to the well known words of Boetius: *Pulchrum pulcherrimus ipse mundum mente gerens, similique ab imagine formans.* Form then, as being in the First Exemplar, is called *idea*; as expressed in matter it is called *paradigma*; and that impression, as imitating the idea, is called an image." *

From this one sees clearly that the degrees are in the perfection of the forms, according to the various expressions of the Divine Being communicated by these forms to corporeal substances.

St. Thomas thus distinguishes them in the second article of his Opusculum *De Formis*, † where the whole doctrine, contained in various parts of his writings, is put together.

"By means of the form," he says, "things come to participate of the Divine Being, and therefore the form also must be a certain participation and likeness of the First Act or Divine Being. . . . So that the nearer this form is in its likeness to the First Act, or the more it participates of His perfections, the more perfect it will be. Therefore the forms that participate of the perfections of the *Actus Primus* merely as to their *being* are of the lowest degree. Those that are like-

---

* *In II. Phys.*, 17.
† This Opusculum *De Formis* was formerly printed as an appendix to St. Thomas's Commentary *In Libros Physicorum*.

nesses of the *Actus Primus* not only by *being*, but also by *living* and being able to give life, have the second rank, under the name of *animæ vegetativæ*. The third are those that are likenesses of the *Actus Primus* not only in having being and life, but also in *knowing*, though imperfectly; and these are named *animæ sensitivæ*. These are the first that have any participation of knowledge. Lastly, those that are likenesses of the *Actus Primus* not only in being and living and having a sort of knowledge, but moreover in knowing with intellective cognition, constitute in nature the highest and noblest grade, though in different ways; and all of these are called intellectual substances."

One can easily conceive how a greater perfection takes into itself inferior perfections, or how an act perfect in itself contains the less perfect acts. Therefore Almighty God, Who is the most perfect Act, has in Himself the perfection of all things created and possible. The more perfect substantial form contains virtually the less perfect, till we come downwards to a form that in its perfection may be called elementary or lowest. So from unity there begins a series, each term of which is endowed with the perfection of the preceding one and something more; so that it tends towards the infinite, which it never can reach.

Thus from the triangle begins a series of polygons, inclining more and more to a polygon with infinite sides, that gives us the conception of the circle, wherein we may find imaged the various perfections of the forms whence the beings in this visible created world, from elements up to man, have their proper perfection.

Since then, according to the principles of this system, every individual being is *one* substance, so the substantial form that makes it one substance must be *one*. And where it is more perfect, as in man, it must contain in itself all the perfections which, apart from man, are communicated by diverse other forms to beings less perfect.

Thus in this system the human soul, through being a form superior to all others in the visible creation, contains in itself virtually their perfection, which it therefore can communicate to matter, while, through being spiritual, it is like the separated substances (the angels), but inferior to all of them, and is as a link that binds the corporeal substances with the incorporeal, the visible with the invisible, a link that joins beings without sense and beings with sense to the order of purely intellectual beings. Therefore it is the most perfect expression made in matter by the First Act, Who is God. It is a divine inspiration, a principle which, though intellectual, can nevertheless transmute the slime of the earth into vegetative and sentient substance. "The soul," says St. Thomas, "is on the confines of the separated substances which are incorporeal, and of the material forms which are corporeal; for it is the lowest of incorruptible forms, ... and therefore is partly separated from matter and partly in matter."*

Hence the essential difference between *materia prima* and the material form and the subsisting form. *Materia prima* is the determinable principle of corporeal substances. The substantial form is the determining principle, the act that constitutes matter in a determinate nature. A substantial form is either inseparable from matter, and is called *material*, or separable from matter, and is called *immaterial*. This quality of being separable from matter is called *subsistence*, and the forms endowed with it are called *subsistent*.

The forms of which we have hitherto spoken are called *substantial*, in contradistinction to those which are called accidental forms; for, as the former constitute substances in their first being as such, so do the latter bring to them, without changing their nature, a second and accidental being.

---

* Opusc. 45, *De Pluralitate Formar.*, P. i.

"Some things that are not, may be," says St. Thomas, "and some already are. That which may be, but is not, is said to be *in potentia*. That which already *is*, is said to be *in actu*. The being of a thing is two-fold,— essential or substantial, such as being a man, which is called Being *simpliciter*, and accidental being, such as a man being white, which is called Being *secundum quid*. . . . That which makes the substantial being *in actu* is called the *substantial form*, and that which makes accidental being *in actu* is called an *accidental form*. And, since generation is motion towards a certain form, as there is a twofold form so is there a twofold generation. Generation absolutely [*simpliciter*] answers to a substantial form. Generation *secundum quid* answers to an accidental form. So that the substantial form of a thing is said to make it be *simpliciter*, as a man comes to be, or is generated; but the accidental form makes it come to be, not *simpliciter*, but in this or that way, as a man who is fair is said to have been born *fair*, in contradistinction to having been born *simpliciter*. This twofold generation implies a twofold corruption, viz. corruption *simpliciter* and corruption *secundum quid*. Simple generation and corruption go not beyond the genus of substance; but generation and corruption *secundum quid* are in all the other genera of accidentals."*

Clearly, then, on the death of a man or a brute or a plant, the substance of the man or of the brute or of the plant ceases to be the substance that it was, as water does when decomposed into its elements. These are examples of absolute corruption ; whereas, when a man loses his colour, the brute its healthiness, the plant its vigour, or the hot water its heat, the substances remain while the accidents change, and the corruption therefore is not a corruption of the substance, but of something that is in the substance.

Hence it follows that matter can pass from one form into another, by reason of not having the form into which it will pass. If the matter, for instance, which now is wheat had already the substantial form of flesh, how could its transformation into flesh be intelligible? When we think of a substance in its actual being, we have only to look at the two principles of matter and form; but if we think of it in its production, we must also consider the privation of that form, by which privation the matter is, so to speak, affected. St. Thomas says: "In order that generation may take place, three things are required, viz. a potential being, which is matter *(materia prima)*; the want of actual being, which is privation;

---
* *Opusc. De Principiis Naturæ.*

and that which makes a thing actually to be, which is the form. Thus, for instance, when an image is made of copper, the copper which is *in potentia* to the form of the image is the matter. The want of figure is privation. The figure that makes it an image is the form. Not, however, a substantial form; for the copper had an actual being previously *as* copper, a being not dependent on having this or that figure. It is an accidental form; and so are all artificial forms, because art works at those things only that have their own natural being. There are three principles of nature therefore, viz. matter, form and privation; the form being that for which generation takes place. The other two belong to the term from which generation is. Hence matter and privation are the same thing in their subject, but differ in our minds; for the same thing that is copper is unfigured before it receives the form of an image, but in one respect is called copper, and in another respect is called unfigured. Wherefore privation is said to be a principle, not *per se* but *per accidens*, because it coincides with the matter."*

Having now considered separately the two principles of every corporeal substance, we shall pass on to consider the same together, as constituting the nature of such.

---
* Ibid.

IV.

NATURE.

THE definition of the word *nature*, as used by the Scholastic doctors, is taken from the second book of Aristotle's *Physics*. "NATURE," he says, "IS THE FIRST PRINCIPLE OF MOTION AND OF REST, *per se*, not *per accidens*." To understand this definition, we must remember that a substance may be moved by an intrinsic or an extrinsic principle. If it is moved by an extrinsic principle, the motion is forced. If it is moved by an intrinsic principle, the motion is natural. When one billiard ball is sent at another, the impulse is extrinsic and the motion forced; but when two drops of mercury, placed near each other, approach and meet, their motion is from an intrinsic principle, and is natural.

This principle is called *nature*. But, besides being a principle of motion, it must also be a principle of rest; for nature inclines things to move, not for the sake of mov·ng, but because it tends to a scope, an end, a *bonum*, which being attained, rest supervenes. Without some obstacle or attraction the motion given to the billiard ball would be perpetual, because it was not directed to a term fixed; whereas the drop of mercury will rest as soon as it has touched the other drop of mercury, to which it is brought by the principle that causes its motion. In this definition of nature, as the principle of motion and of rest, the words *prima* and *per se*, contradistinctive to *per accidens*, are put to distinguish the principle whence the motion proceeds (which is *nature*) from any modification or accidental affection of it, without which it would either not be set in motion towards the object, or inclined with a different intensity — a very valuable distinction in Catholic theology for distinguishing nature from grace and the natural from the supernatural. And this much will suffice about the physical meaning of the word *nature*.

Let us now see what constitutes it in a corporeal substance. In this there is matter and form. Matter alone would not be sufficient, because matter *(materia prima)* remains the same under all substantial forms, and therefore, were it *per se* a principle of operation, it would always operate in one way. But that does not happen. Oxygen, for instance, and water are different in their operation, though all the matter *(materia prima)* that is in one is likewise in the other. Does the substantial form, then, constitute the nature of corporeal substance? If we consider the matter as *per se* inert, and the form as the only other thing in corporeal substances, we must say that the form is the principle of operation or of motion. But would it be so, if it were separated from the matter? No, for it could not exist at all. And therefore, to be the principle of operation and of motion, it must be united with matter. The word *nature* does indeed principally apply to it, but not with propriety as prescinding from the matter which it informs. Rightly therefore did Aristotle say in the second book of *Physics*, that as copper, if we prescind from its figure, cannot be called art, neither can matter *(materia prima)*, when considered apart from the substantial form which determines it to a certain species, be called the nature of a thing; but that name should rather be given to the form.* "As that may be called art," says St. Thomas, "which belongs to anything that is according to art and artificial, so may that be called nature which belongs to anything that is according to nature and natural. But that which is only *in potentia* to be made by man's art cannot be said to have anything of art in it, because it has not as yet the nature of (for instance) a bed. Therefore in natural things that which is flesh and bone in *potentia* has not the nature of flesh and bone

---

* *Phys.*, Lib. ii. Cap. i.

till it has received the form, according to which is the definite nature of the thing, and through which we know what flesh is and what bone is. There is no nature in it till it has its form; and therefore the form is in a way the nature of natural things that have in them the principle of motion." †

From this we can easily understand why the Scholastics called matter and form incomplete substances, and the *compositum* a complete substance. For that being which naturally is of itself is a substance; and matter cannot be of itself without the form, nor can a material form (for of that we are here speaking) be without matter. True it is that neither the one nor the other can be called an accident, because each has its own entity; but when disjoined they are wanting in what is required for the definition of substance, and therefore are incomplete. This they acquire when conjoined; and then they are a complete substance. "We call a substance physically incomplete," says Suarez in his *Metaphysics*, "that by its entity has not in itself what is required for the nature of substance taken generically; and that which has it we call a complete substance. This we express by means of negation, saying that a substance is physically complete which is *not* ordained *per se*

---
† *In II. Phys.*, lect. 2.

to perfect or to constitute with another substance another being." *

And Cicero speaks likewise in these words: *De natura autem ita dicebant* (Aristotle and his followers) *ut eam dividerent in res duas, ut altera esset efficiens, altera, quasi huic se præbens, ea quæ efficeretur aliquid. In eo quod efficeret, vim esse censebant: in eo autem quod efficeretur materiam quamdam: in utroque tamen utrumque. Neque enim materiam ipsam cohærere potuisse, si nulla vi contineretur, neque vim sine aliqua materia. Nihil est enim quod non alicubi esse cogatur. Sed quod ex utroque; id jam corpus nominabant.* †

Here it is evident that, since what he calls *vim* cannot be without matter, nor matter without form, each is an incomplete substance, and the body alone, composed of the two, is a complete substance.

Moreover, if the substantial form principally constitutes the nature, clear it is that plurality of such forms brings plurality of natures. Hence a body can never be considered as one nature, if it be nothing more than an aggregate of atoms, each furnished with its own substantial form. Even a man could not be said to have one complete nature, if there were in him more than one substantial form; for with

---
* *Disp.*, 33, Sect. 1. n. 3.   † *Acad.*, i. 6.

each form he would have a complete nature. And therefore St. Thomas argues thus: "One thing results from many things, firstly according to order alone, as a city is made of many houses, or an army is made of many soldiers; and secondly by order and composition, as a house is made by contact and junction of parts. But these two ways do not suffice to constitute out of many things one nature; and therefore those things that have a common form in order or in composition are not natural things, whose unity can be called the unity of nature."* And therefore, if we 'suppose a body as formed by mere aggregation of atoms or molecules, we cannot call it one in nature, though all its parts concur in one operation as to the term. One nature implies not only one term, but also one principle of operation, which cannot be where many operating things have a divided being. "It is impossible," says St. Thomas, "that there can be one operation in things which differ in their being. I say *one*, not on the part of that in which the action terminates, but as it comes from the agent; for many men dragging a boat do *one* work as to the thing done, which is one, but on the part of the men who drag it the actions are many, because the impulses that move the boat are many." †

---

* *Contra Gent.*, iv. 35.   † *Contra Gent.*, ii. 57.

Nor can it be said that we may suppose each atom to be an incomplete nature which is completed by the aggregation of many atoms; for from what we have shown about the two natures (the complete and the incòmplete), it is evident that each atom would really be a complete substance and nature, and therefore that the whole would only have a collective unity.

We say this because it is important to make the meaning of the word *nature* quite clear, seeing that it is not always in these times as clear as in the days of old. Any one may see how necessary it is to be clear about this. If there were no other reason, the Catholic definitions concerning man, and above all, concerning the Divine Word Incarnate, ought to be sufficient.

V.

CREATION.

TO show the unity, beauty and majesty of the Physical System, we must consider it, as far as the nature of this treatise will allow, in its principal relations ; and creation is certainly one of them. For this purpose we shall here quote the words of a most sublime genius, where he interprets the first chapter of Genesis. What is that void and formless earth, and the darkness, and the abysses, and the waters, and the Spirit of God moving over it, of which we read in that divine book ? " The Spirit of God," says St. Augustine, " moved over the water. It was not yet said that God made the water; nor can we believe that the water was not made by God, nor that it was before He had formed anything. For by Him, through Him and in Him are all things, as the Apostle says. Therefore God did make the water, and we cannot say otherwise without being greatly in error. Why then is it not said that God made the water ? Did He give the name of water to that same matter which He called heaven and earth, earth invisible and uncomposed, and an abyss? Why should it not be called water, if it could be called earth, when neither earth nor water nor anything was distinct? But perhaps, and not incongruously, it was first called heaven and earth, then uncomposed earth, and an abyss without light, and lastly water. Firstly, to indicate, under the name of heaven and earth, the matter of the universe, to form which it was all taken out of nothing. Secondly, to show, under the names of uncomposed earth, and of an abyss, the nudity of forms [*informitas*], because the earth is the most unformed and least splendid of those things. Thirdly, to signify under the name of water that matter is obedient to the artificer; for water is more pliant than earth, and therefore matter, by reason of being pliant, was better expressed by the word 'water' than by the word 'earth.' . . . This way of signifying matter shows firstly the end, or why it was made, secondly the formlessness, thirdly the dependence on and subjection to the artificer. To the first, then, belong 'heaven and earth,' for which precisely matter was made. To the second belong the words, 'invisible and uncomposed earth,' and ' darkness over the abyss,' or formlessness without light, wherefore it was called invisible earth. To the third belongs 'the water subject to the Spirit,' and receiving therefrom order and forms. Thus the Spirit of God moved over the waters; whereby we may understand that the Spirit operated, and that water was the matter of His operation."* We can therefore conceive, in accordance with the saint, an immense ocean, as it were, of we know not what entity, as yet without any definite nature, so that it could be truly called neither water, nor air, nor ether, nor anything that is considered in physics. It was not divided into atoms nor determined in certain figures any more than the darkness that represents it was divided into colours. It only gives us that primitive matter which God created as the indeterminate subject, capable of receiving in itself the images of the divine archetypal ideas, which, as we showed in the third chapter, the substantial forms are.

This is how the Spirit of God (which means God Himself) applies Himself, as we may say, to this formless water, or rather primitive matter, and infuses into it His own virtue, so that in it and with it in ways innumerable He expresses Himself in more or less perfect degrees, just as a sculptor (to use a weak similitude) might express in modelling clay his own image, not by an instrument, but by the application of himself, that leaves a greater or less impress here and there.

---

* *De Gen.*, ad litt. i. c. 2.

God, being infinite, cannot express Himself adequately otherwise than in His Word, Whom He generates, and Who has the same nature. In matter, whether the whole or a part, He cannot be expressed. Hence, though the grades of creatures in the corporeal universe are almost innumerable, according to the various perfections imparted to them by their forms, these creatures reflect only a very feeble ray from that ACTUS PURISSIMUS which God is; and so does every other created being, however sublime and perfect. This is expressed by Dante, in the *Paradiso :*

> Colui che volse il sesto
> Allo stremo del mondo, e dentro ad esso
> Distinse tanto occulto e manifesto,
> Non poteò suo valor si fare impresso
> In tutto l'Universo, che il suo Verbo
> Non rimanesse in infinito eccesso.
>
> * * * *
> E quinci appar ch' ogni minor natura
> È corto recettacolo a quel bene
> Che non ha fine e sè con sè misura. *

And in Canto xxix. he says:

> Vedi l'eccelso omai e la larghezza
> Dell' eterno Valor, poscia che tanti
> Speculi fatti s'ha, in che si spezza,
> Uno manendo in sè come davanti.

St. Augustine goes on to explain the self-application of God in forming matter to His own image. "And the Spirit of God," he

---
* *Il Paradiso*, canto xix.

says, " bore Himself over the water, not as oil floats on water .... but with a certain effective and making virtue [*vi quadam effectoria et fabricatoria*], by which that over which He bears Himself is made and constructed, as the will of an artificer acts on the wood or other material on which he works, or on the limbs of his own body when he moves them to the work. But this, though the best of corporeal similitudes, is poor and almost nothing as intended to make us understand how the Spirit of God bore Himself above the mundane matter subject to His operation. Yet, among those things that may somehow be understood by men, we cannot find a similitude that could be more clearly understood, or more nearly resemble that of which we have spoken." *

It will be objected that, if *materia prima* is at first formless and then formed, we must admit an entity which has neither the nature of earth nor of water nor of anything else; an entity which has no nature at all, or, as they say in the Schools, is not *quid* ; an entity which has no determinate figure, and therefore is not *quantum* ; an entity which has no attributes, no accidents, no quality of any sort, and therefore is not *quale*. This, it will be said, is inconceivable. Now, if the doctrine were that God created *materia prima* first *in order of*

---
* *De Gen.*, ad litt. ibid. 16.

time, and afterwards determined it in various natures by impression of forms, assuredly such a *nec quid, nec quantum, nec quale*, standing by itself, would be inconceivable and extremely unnatural, if not absurd. But, when we are told that in creation *materia prima* preceded the forms *in order of nature only, and not in order of time*, the difficulty vanishes, as St. Augustine explains with his usual profoundness. "Hast Thou not taught me, O Lord," he says, "that before this formless matter was formed and distinguished by Thee, there was nothing at all—no colour, no figure, no body, no spirit? Not however quite nothing, but a certain informity without a species of any sort. . . Nor will this appear inconsistent to any one who can distinguish between the precedence of eternity, of time, of election and of origin—between eternal precedence, as God precedes all things; precedence in time, as the flower precedes its fruit; precedence by election, as the fruit is preferred to the flower; and precedence by origin, as the sound precedes the singing. Of these examples the first and last are very difficult to understand; but the others are very easy. For indeed it is an arduous work, and very rarely done, to raise one's eyes to Thine Eternity, O Lord, which, being incommutable, makes the mutable things, and therefore precedes them.

And then, who is sufficiently acute to discern without much labour how the sound is before the singing, seeing that the singing is the sound formed (distinct in certain forms), and that, although there can be a thing unformed, what *is not* cannot receive a form? Thus matter is before that which is made of it, but not first, as the efficient cause; for it does not make, but rather is made. Nor is it first by an interval of time; for even in singing we do not first emit unformed sounds, and then give them the order and form of singing, as when a man makes a casket out of wood or a vase out of silver. The wood and the silver precede in time the form of a casket and of a vase: but in singing it is not so. What we hear is not firstly an unformed sound, that passes away when formed, and leaves nothing behind for art to recover. It is the very sound of the singing itself; and therefore the singing developes in the sound, which is its own sound, its own matter formed into song. Hence, as I said, the matter of the sound is prior to the form of the song: not prior by efficiency, for the sound does not make the song; but by being subject to the soul that produces the song. Neither is it prior in time; for it comes forth together with the song. Nor is it prior by choice; for sound is not preferable to song, which is a sound and also a beautiful sound.

It is prior by priority of origin; for the form is not given to make the song a sound, but to make the sound a song. Let this example serve to show, before those who can understand, how the matter of things was made first, and called heaven and earth, because heaven and earth were made of it, but not made first in time, because the forms give the order of time, and the matter was unformed."*

The holy doctor then exclaims: "May Thy works praise Thee, that we may love Thee; and may we love Thee, that so Thy works may praise Thee—those works which have in time their beginning and end, their rising and setting, their perfection and defect, form and privation. They had therefore successively morning and evening, partly hidden and partly manifest; for by Thee they were made from nothing, not of Thee, nor of anything not Thine, nor of anything anterior in time, but of matter concreated, by Thee created together with them; because Thou, without interval of time, didst give form to the formlessness of this matter, the matter of heaven and earth being other than the form of heaven and earth, Thou tookest the matter absolutely from nothing, and from formless matter the form of the world. Yet both didst Thou make together, so that

---
* *Confess.* xii. 3, 40.

without the interposition of a moment the form followed the matter."*

But we have said enough about the outcoming of primitive matter by the power of God, and about its distinction in those primitive substantial forms from which the development of the universe came successively. We have now to see what happens in the actuation of this matter in the diverse forms that distinguish it.

* Ibid. xiii. 48

VI.

ATOMS.

THE word "atom," used by Democritus and Epicurus, Descartes and Gassendi, to signify the smallest possible substance, means rather that which is undivided, and cannot while preserving its nature be divided. This definition implies the notion of individuality, as Cicero says; and, since it prescinds *per se* from size, a large body might sometimes be called an atom, while a smaller one could not. This being premised, let us consider what an atom is in the system that we are explaining.

As a seal can multiply its own image by impressing any sealing-wax whatsoever, so can the divine archetypal idea multiply the divine image in matter according to the number of impressions that God makes on it. From this it clearly appears that universality belongs to the idea, and that singularity and individuality come from the matter on which it is impressed, as St. Thomas lays down in these often repeated words: *Individuatio formæ est ex materia, per quam forma contrahitur ad hoc determinatum.* * Now this impression on

---
* Quodlib. vii. 3.

matter is in the manner of a virtue derived from God; and the substantial form determines an individual being in its nature. Hence it evidently is not and cannot be made in divided and separated matter, because in that case the form would not be *one*, but as many as the parts of the disjointed matter. Therefore an individual corporeal substance is continuous—is an atom. The size of it will depend on the form, which may require more or less extension in the matter, or be itself indifferent as to that. Thus an individual man is a substance in his continuous extension, not an aggregate of minute bodies divided and separated. For otherwise the human soul, which is the substantial form of human beings, would be in itself divided and separated; and instead of one soul there would in fact be as many souls as there would be little bodies of which we should suppose ourselves to be constituted. The same may be said of an individual brute, and of an individual plant, and of any inanimate substance that is individual. So that, if the word *atom* is to mean an individual corporeal substance, we may call by that name not only a little inanimate substance, but even a plant, a brute or a man. Whence it follows that in the one and the same substance the so-called physical pores, i.e. interstices placed all round each atom, or, as they call it, each corporeal substance of the smallest dimensions, cannot be admitted in the physical system, because they would take away the unity of the individual. But the pores that we do find in corporeal substances do not take away the unity of the subject; and they must be acknowledged, because experience proves that they are.

An atom, understood in the strict sense of the word, requires also indivisibility, not absolute but relative, owing to which the substance called "atom" cannot be divided without ceasing to be what it is. This does not prejudice the indefinite divisibility of matter; for that regards extension as considered by reason of the quantity, not by reason of the nature in which it inheres. The relative indivisibility of matter is especially observable in living things, that will not bear division while retaining the nature of their being, because they have a form that requires a certain organism not to be had in every small quantity of matter. Generally all corporeal substances have a *minimum*, that cannot be less without ceasing to exist, and therefore may deservedly be called an atom according to the strictest meaning of the word.

But will two individual substances, or atoms, that occupy an equal space, have in themselves an equal quantity of matter? And, without increase of the matter, can the same substance occupy more space than before, or occupy less without diminishing it? This question belongs to the doctrine about the mass and volume of the atom; the volume meaning the place occupied by the atom, or its extension with respect to space, and the said volume being either real or apparent. The place, for instance, which a plant seems to occupy is the apparent, not the real volume; for, although the plant has in all its living substance a true continuation, it yet contains innumerable interstices or pores, in which the substance is not. If it were there, the volume would be not merely apparent, but real. The matter intrinsic to the plant constitutes its mass.

This being laid down, the followers of the physical system said that two substances occupying an equal space can have different masses, or a different mass in equal real volumes, and that the same substance may have, without increase of mass, a real volume sometimes more and sometimes less. We remember showing in the year 1878 in the "Civiltà Cattolica" (Serie x. vol. vi. p. 73) that an argument of Galileo's, to prove the variability of real volumes, had no force : but disapproving of the argument in favour of a thing is very different from disapproving of the opinion itself. Epicurus and Descartes did disapprove of it, for they acknowledged no other density and rarity than what arises from more or less distance between the atoms, and affirmed their extension to be immutable. Cardinal Toledo explains the teaching of Aristotle and of St. Thomas about it in these words: "That which contains little matter in much quantity is called rare. . . . That which contains much matter in little quantity is dense. . . . We have to remember that there is a twofold rarefaction and condensation, proper and improper. Improper rarefaction or condensation is what happens by mere approximation or segregation of parts, without any change or alteration of them, . . . and this [improper rarefaction or condensation] does not take place unless an external body is expelled or introduced. Many among the ancients acknowledged no other than this; but they supposed quite vacant pores in bodies, while we affirm them to be full of a most subtle corporeal substance. . . . Proper rarefaction and condensation is not produced by expelling or introducing an extraneous body, but by an internal change of the subject."* Here we have a change of extension. The matter remains the same.

This suggests a natural explanation of the greater or less gravity that substances acquire by change of position. In fact, if part of a solid body be divided and subdivided ever

---
* *In IV. Phys.*, C. 9, Q. 11.

so much by purely mechanical means, it will not be lighter than before; but it really would be so, if properly rarified, so that in rising it made room for the other part of the same body, which was not rarified, and which has more matter under an equal real volume. We say "of the same body," because we must admit that a corporeal substance in a liquid state may be more dense and contain more matter than another corporeal substance in a solid state. This variation of gravity is explained by St. Thomas, according to the doctrine of Aristotle, as follows: "The size of a body is extended or simplified in rarefaction, not by the matter receiving into itself any other thing, but because the matter which first was *in potentia* to be greater or less becomes actually so; and therefore the substance is not made rare or dense by addition or substraction of extraneous particles, but by the matter itself becoming rare or dense. . . . He [Aristotle] proves his assertion by the effects of the rare and the dense; for the difference between the heavy and the light, the hard and the soft, follows the difference between rarity and density. . . He says therefore that the lightness of bodies is in consequence of their rarity, the heaviness in consequence of their density. And he is right; for the rarity of a substance comes from the matter receiving greater dimensions, and its density is because the matter has less dimensions. Hence, if, of two bodies equal in extension, the one is rare and the other dense, the dense body has the most matter." * These considerations deserve to be weighed and examined, not despised.

According to this doctrine it follows that corporeal substances, unless impeded by an extrinsic motive power or other obstacle, will be so disposed around centres of gravity that the more dilated bodies will go further and further from them. Therefore, if all round the earth, for instance, various spaces be supposed in the manner of concentric spherical strata, each corporeal substance would have its own, in proportion to its density, from the densest even to the most subtle ether, whose density is so slight that we can hardly form a conception of it.

And consequently we have to admit that an ethereal and most subtle bodily substance is everywhere diffused in the interplanetary spaces, as the vehicle and subject of the reciprocal operation of the stars and the planets, though these are placed at such enormous distances from each other. Thus without contradicting the indisputable axiom, *Non datur actio in distans*, we can explain the diffusion of light and heat in agreement with experience.

---

* *In IV. Phys.*, lect. 14.

On the contrary, they who, following Epicurus and Descartes, affirm the existence of equally impenetrable atoms unalterable in their extension, are compelled thereby to admit in nature much more of absolute void than of space occupied by corporeal substances. They have to suppose ethereal atoms at a great distance from each other, and thus make inexplicable (according to the true system of irradiation) not alone the extreme rapidity of the propagation of light, but even the fact of its propagation. God, however, Who willed order and unity in the corporeal universe, and made substances to act on other substances in the most various and admirable ways, so ordained that there are substances whose nature it is to dilate and rarify in the highest degree and fill the vast spaces of the heavens, passing between the interstices of bodies almost incredibly small. This is what is meant by the very old adage, *Natura abhorret a vacuo*. We should be indulgent to the old physicists who explained by this adage such phenomena as the rising of water in curved tubes, and so on; but the modern physicists have no right to maintain that the Torricellian vacuum refutes the adage. The old adage refers to an *absolute* vacuum, while the vacuum obtained by art is imperfect and relative.

We have now to pass on from the

consideration of corporeal substances, in their individual and absolute being, to consider them in those mutual relations that have their foundation and origin in the seminal causes.

VII.

SEMINAL CAUSES.

IN creating actuated matter by substantial forms God produced also what may be called the seminal causes of things, which enable substances to produce others like or unlike themselves. Strictly speaking, however, this term expresses the virtue communicated by God to a living substance, and through it to its seed, by which it generates another substance of the same species. Furthermore it expresses the virtue by which even things without life are the causes of substantial change. "From that which is more perfect," says St. Thomas, "the denominations of things are taken. Now the most perfect of all corporeal substances are living substances . . But evidently the seeds from which they are generated are their active and passive principle; and therefore all the active and passive virtues that are principles of generation and of natural changes are suitably called by St. Augustine *(3 De Trinitate) seminales rationes.* The active and passive virtues may be considered in a manifold order. Firstly, as St. Augustine says,* they are principally and originally in the very Word of God, as ideal essences. Secondly, they are in the elements of the world, where from the beginning they were produced at once, as universal causes. In a third way they are found in those things that out of universal causes are in course of time produced, for instance, in this plant or that animal, as in particular causes. In a fourth way they are in the seeds produced by animals and plants.† . . . Without these seminal virtues, given by God, the living things first created would have disappeared from the earth, and that continual transformation of substances, which is so necessary for the maintenance of such, would have ceased.

This most wise providence of the Creator is thus described by St. Thomas: "The coming forth of creatures from God is like the coming forth of artistic works from an artist; and therefore, as artificial forms in matter proceed from the artificer, so do natural forms and virtues descend from the ideas in the Divine Mind. . . . But the works of God differ in two respects from those of the artificer. Firstly, on the part of the matter; for the artificer does not produce that, but works on it, and never could give to it the power of

---

* 6 *De Gen.*, ad litt. † *Summa*, P. i. Q. cxv. a. 2.

receiving those forms which he communicates thereto; but God, Who is the cause of all being, not only gave to things their forms and natural being, but also communicated to matter *(materia prima)* the power of receiving whatever He may please to operate in it. Secondly, on the part of the forms; for the forms introduced by the artificer are not able to produce a being like themselves. A wooden bed cannot bring forth another wooden bed, though, if reduced to ashes, it may help to form a plant; but the natural forms can produce the same things, and therefore have the property of seed, in virtue of which they may be called seminal." *

Having thus given a general sketch of the Physical System as to the generation of things, we must now descend to the particular, and apply it to the various kinds of corporeal substances. Some living things have only vegetative life, and others have sensitive life also. The former are called plants, the latter animals. God gave to the primitive animals the above mentioned seminal virtue, but so that in the one sex it should be an active principle, in the other passive, and that the seminal substance communicated by the genitors should have life, not actually, but virtually, as having the power to produce,

---
* *In II. Sent.*, Dist. xviii. 1, 2.

under requisite circumstances, a living thing. In such generation therefore there is no creation, properly so called; for the *anima sensitiva* is caused by the originating seminal virtue, which, though simple in itself, is yet material, as being so tied to matter that it can neither operate nor exist separate therefrom. Of course we are prescinding from man, because the human soul is immaterial, and therefore, even when separated, can exist and operate. "God has not given to corporeal substances," says St. Thomas, "by means of the seminal virtues, the means of producing a human soul; but He has given to brutes the power of so producing the *anima sensitiva*. And this," he adds, "the Sacred Scripture seems to indicate in the book of Genesis. There, speaking of the origin of other animals, it ascribes their souls to other causes, saying *Producant aquæ reptile animæ viventis*, &c. * But, when speaking of man, it shows that his soul was immediately created by God; for it says that God formed man of the slime of the earth, and breathed into his face the breath of life." † And here we must remark that the conjunction of the two seminal principles in every living thing is called conception, and is prior in time to the production and existence of the vital principle or soul, which

---
* *Gen.*, i. 20.   † *Met.*, vii.

is called animation. It is absurd and against facts to suppose that the conception and the animation are simultaneous.

The same thing is to be said of plants; for God conferred on them similar virtues, and they confer those virtues on the seminal substances, so that the one gives the active, and the other the passive seminal principle, which, being conjoined, give the completed seed, not living actually, but having efficient power of life. When there is no distinction of sex one part of the same plant gives the active principle, and the other the passive. "Those [animals]," St. Thomas says, "that have perfect life have also a perfect generation, and therefore are distinguished as active and passive. But it is not so in the imperfect life that plants have; for in the same plant there is the twofold virtue, active and passive, though sometimes the active is found in one, and the passive in another, so that the one plant is said to be masculine and the other feminine."

Clearly then the distinction of sex in plants is not a recent discovery of modern science, as some people would have it to be. Here we must remark, by the way, that, if any human being could by chemical art determine with certainty the elements of which the seminal substance of living beings is composed, and

---
* *Comm. in III. Sent.*, Dist. iii. Q. ii. a. 1.

combine them so as to make of it a substance quite similar materially to the completed seed, the substance would nevertheless have no seminal virtue, because it would not proceed from living parents. And therefore if, *per impossibile*, it were possible for any man to produce by art the organism of a plant or of a brute, he could never produce a live brute or a live plant.

The two principles of seminal virtue for the generation of animals and plants may, by analogy, be said to be required for the production of a new substance in beings without life. Oxygen and hydrogen will not produce water, although put together in the right proportions, unless there is some extrinsic cause to modify their virtue, so that their mutual action may produce a change of one relative principle into another, thereby constituting the nature of water. Evidently these elementary substances are different from non-elementary or mixed substances. The elementary substances do not result from the union of two other substances; but by physically uniting they produce a new substance in a different nature, viz. mixed substances. But why do we call these *mixed*, when in natural sciences now they are called *composite*, and the word *mixed* is used to signify a mixture? The reason is, that since every corporeal substance is composed of matter and form, the name of composite belongs as much to the elementary as to the non-elementary; so that a mixed substance cannot properly be called a mixture, but only two or more substances locally mingled by aggregation, each keeping its primary nature. The word *mixed* belongs of right to that only which is produced by physical union, so that from two or more substances there results one substance only.

And, since anything may be resolved into the elements of which it is constituted, any mixed substance (say water) may be resolved into its component parts. Aristotle, explaining as a philosopher the inmost nature of elements, tells us* that an element of bodies is that substance which is obtained by resolution of others, and which cannot be resolved into another of a different species. St. Thomas, commenting on him, says: "An element of other bodies is that into which those other bodies are decomposed or resolved; for not every cause may be called an element, but only that which enters into the composition of a thing."† Again he says: "In natural corporeal substances, those into which all mixed bodies resolve themselves are called elements of bodies; and consequently they are those from which the mixed bodies result. And the bodies called elements are not divided into

---
* iii. *De Cælo et Mundo.* † Lect. viii.

others differing from each other in species, but into similar parts."* Hence he calls elementary bodies "simple." "Elementary bodies," he says "are simple, and there is no composition in them except that of matter and form."† Following this doctrine, Toledo says: "In two ways we may conclude that elementary substances are. Firstly, from the dissolution of bodies; it being a fact that some decompose into bodies of a different nature, and others into bodies of the same nature. The resolved parts are evidently composed of those into which they do resolve; and an infinite process of resolving is repugnant to reason. Therefore, there must be bodies that are not resolved into others, or, in other words, elementary bodies. Secondly, we may conclude this likewise from composition. For we know that many bodies are made by mixture (now called chemical combination); but elementary bodies cannot be so made. Therefore those really are simple bodies, which do not result from composition of others." ‡

Such is the doctrine professed in the system before us; but it does not claim to determine how many and which the elementary bodies are. These have been supposed to be four, and thought to be twenty or fifty, and now

---
* *In V. Met.*, 3.   † *Contra Gent.*, iii. 23.
‡ Lib. ii. *De Generat. et corrupt.*, Q. 4.

54 THE PHYSICAL SYSTEM OF ST. THOMAS.

the amount is over eighty ; nor can any one say how many they may be found to be. By means of reasoning we can only affirm with Toledo that "the elements are more than one."* That much we can affirm ; for otherwise the production of new natures would be impossible, because the union of two equal things cannot constitute something of a different species. The atomic theory, therefore, cannot be true ; because, according to that doctrine, the atoms are all of the same nature. Experiment, not reason, determines which and how many elementary substances cooperate in forming this or that mixed body ; and even experiment does not, after so many centuries, give with certainty a final settlement of that question.

In defending the old teachers from unjust attacks, men of high ability and great learning, such as the distinguished philosopher, Cardinal Battaglini, and the famous Professor Lorenzelli, have in their philosophical courses given another meaning to the word "elements ;" but we prefer to avoid troublesome and unnecessary disputation. We simply say that since the old teachers, when teaching as philosophers, tell us that elements or elementary bodies are those bodies of which mixed bodies are composed, and which result from the decomposition of the latter, we have a

---
* Ibid., iii.

right to use the same correct definition in experimental physics, for the purpose of seeing what bodies are such—whether solid, liquid, fluid, or aerial. Modern chemists cannot deny that; for with them the element is the first in chemical synthesis and the last in chemical analysis.

VIII.

QUALITIES.

OF these very little is said in modern schools of physics or of philosophy; and yet the doctrine about it is so important, that without it the physical system would be untenable, and all nature would appear to the mind to be full, not only of inexplicable puzzles, but also of evident contradictions. Let us begin by asking this question: Suppose that we acknowledge the complete and highest Being of God, yet deny His operation. What could we then say about His knowing, loving, creating? What sort of conception could we form of that most perfect Nature? Either none at all, or the conception of an absurdity.

As God is the complete and most perfect Being *(esse)*, so in Him there is not any real difference between being and the power to do and the action itself. He is the One most pure, most simple, most complete, most perfect ACT. But it is not so with created substances, especially corporeal ones, with which we are now more particularly concerned. They have indeed a likeness to God, inasmuch as they have being, and have power to act, and do act; but, by reason of their imperfection, there necessarily is a real distinction between their being, their power to act and their action. Moreover, since God is most perfect and the source of all being, He never can receive from His creatures anything intrinsic to Himself, nor can they take from Him anything of His own. In other words, He cannot receive that inner mutation which is philosophically called *passio*, and which in its general meaning denotes a change made in a substance by the action of some being.

This being premised as the basis of the following dissertation, let us consider any finite substance: and since it is easier to descend from the more perfect to the less, when the more perfect is known to us, we shall begin with man. Now by mentally abstracting from man all action, all passion, every faculty, what remains of him? The bare essence of the human individual, as constituted by the soul substantially informing the corporeal matter. Whatever therefore we may conceive as happening to him when thus constituted and determined, will not be a substantial form that determines his nature, but an accidental form, which adds nothing more than *quality*. Therefore, remembering that besides human nature with its natural faculties, man has dispositions that adorn it and make it fitter for action, we must acknowledge that these are true qualities.

When a man acts either with his intellect or with his will, or with any other power that he has, there certainly happens to him a modification that before was not; and this is a quality. And, when at the sight of an object, pleasing or otherwise, he receives in his senses and in his soul an impression that was not there before, this, too, is a quality. Lastly, the human soul, as the substantial form, is the determining principle of the substances that nourish man to become part of his nature; and thus it gives in various ways to the body a certain extension, quantity and figure. Here again there is quality. We can therefore distinguish four species of quality, of which the first belongs to Being; the second to action; the third to passion; the fourth to quantity. "Properly speaking," says St. Thomas, "quality means a certain mode of substance. . . . Now the mode, or the determination of the subject, according to accidental Being, may be understood either according to the nature of the subject, or in reference to action, or to passion, (these proceed from the principles of nature which are matter and form,) or according to quantity. If we take the mode or determination of the subject according to quantity, we have the fourth species of quality. . . . The mode or determination of the subject according to action and passion gives the second and third species of quality. . . . But the mode or determination of the subject according to the nature of the thing belongs to the first species of quality. * . . . This does not contradict what he lays down in his commentary on the Sentences, where he says that the *compositum* does not operate in virtue of the matter, but of the form, which is its *actus* and principle of action. "The quantity," he says, "belongs to matter, the quality to Form." † For it is not affirmed that the said species of quality is quantity itself. It is the determination that is in the composite being under this or that quantity; and though the quantity belongs to matter, the determination is by virtue of the form.

Of the species inferior to man, whether they have life or have not, we must consider firstly their substantial being: secondly, what is accidental in them, constituted by the four different species of quality before mentioned. If an atom of oxygen, for instance, receives into itself a disposition which it previously had not, it will have a quality of the first species: and being in fact able to operate on another by attracting or altering, it will have a modification that contains the quality of the

---

* *Summa*, 1a. 2æ. Q. xlix. 2. † Bk. xii. iv. Q. 1.

second species. If instead of that, it receives into itself the operation of another, it will acquire through the change undergone a quality of the third species. Lastly, if by virtue of an extrinsic cause, its proper quantity comes to be so determined that it acquires a different conformation of parts, that quality will belong to the fourth species.

We must observe that all the corporeal substances of equal matter have substantial forms, which, though differing from each other in perfection, have something in common, as we have seen by the comparison that Aristotle and St. Thomas took from geometrical figures and numbers. As in every polygon there is the triangle, and in every number there is unity, so in every substantial form there is an inferior or elementary form, not formally but virtually. This applies to qualities also, which, as we have said, are in being by reason of form. Hence the lowest qualities of the lowest elementary substance are common to all the superior substances. Thus, for instance, we find that attraction and gravitation, subjection to heat, expansion and the rest, are common to all corporeal substances. Since then a more perfect being has a substantial form that contains the perfections of the inferior forms, it must also possess their qualities. But as in a *one* being all must be in harmony and order, so even in the qualities, there is a certain law by which, where the inferior qualities would clash with the superior, the inferior are there in a remitted degree, or, in modern language, diminished or neutralized. "We must hold with the philosopher (Aristotle)," says St. Thomas, "that the forms of the elements remain in the mixture, not actually, but virtually. The qualities of the elements properly remain, though remitted; and in them appears the virtue of the elementary forms."*

And now, to make the whole theory of the system clear as to the gradation in the modes operating and the qualities of all beings, we cannot do better than quote another grand passage from the Angelic Doctor, where he reduces it to order and unity, giving us a sure foundation of rational physics.

"There is nothing," he says, "that more immediately and intimately belongs to things than Being; and therefore, since matter is actuated by form, the form that gives being to the matter must be conceived as coming to it first of all things, and most intimately Now it is a property of the substantial form that it gives being absolutely to matter; FOR THE SUBSTANTIAL FORM IS THAT BY WHICH A THING IS WHAT IT IS. The accidental forms do not give being absolutely, but in one

---

* *Summa*, P. i. Q. lxxvi. a. 4 ad 4.

respect, such as being great, or coloured, etc. Hence, if there is a form that does not give being to matter absolutely, but comes to matter already actuated by some form, it will not be substantial. Hence it is evident that between substantial form and matter there cannot be any intermediate substantial form (as some will have it) supposing that, according to the order of *genera*, of which one is under the other, there is an order of diverse forms in matter: as, for instance, that matter has the being of actual substance from one form, the being of corporeal substance from another, the being of an animated body from another, and so on. But according to that position the first form only, by which the actual being of substance was given, would be substantial. All the others would be accidental; for the substantial form, as we have already said, is that which constitutes the determinate being, *(quæ facit hoc aliquid.)* We must therefore say that one and the same form is that by which a thing is a determinate substance and by which it is determined in its ultimate species (specialissima), and in all the intermediate genera," (by which, for example, a man is a man and an animal and a living creature and a corporeal substance). " Consequently, since the forms of natural things are like numbers, in which the addition and subtraction of a unit makes a different species, we must understand that the diversity of natural forms, according to which the matter is constituted in different species, is because one form adds a greater perfection. For instance, one form constitutes a substance in corporeal being only. . . . Another and more perfect form constitutes matter in vital as well as in corporeal being. And then another form gives to it not only corporeal and vital being, but also sensitive being, and so forth. We must see therefore that the more perfect form, inasmuch as simultaneously with the matter it constitutes the *compositum* in the perfection of an inferior grade, must be understood as material with respect to an ulterior perfection, and so on. Thus *materia prima*, as constituted in corporeal being, is matter with respect to the ulterior perfection of that which has life. Hence (logically) the body is the *genus* of the living body, and its being animated or living is the *differentia*. For the *genus* is as the matter, the *differentia* is as the form; and thus in a manner one and the same form, as actuating matter in a lower grade, is midway between the matter and itself as actuating it in a higher grade. Matter understood as constituted in substantial being according to the perfection of an inferior grade, must consequently be supposed as subject to accidents. For a substance in that lower grade of perfection must have certain accidents proper to itself." . . . .

"Thus, when we say that man is a corporeal substance, living, sensitive and rational, we do not mean that he is constituted in these diverse grades by diverse forms. We mean that the perfect form, the soul, which makes him rational, makes him a sensitive substance also, and a living substance and a corporeal substance; for since every superior grade presupposes the inferior, the human soul as constituting the rational grade, presupposes itself as constituting the sensitive grade, or sensitive being (*esse*) with its accidents and qualities; and so on."

St. Thomas goes on to say: "Since then the soul is the substantial form, as constituting man in a determinate species of substance, there is no substantial form between the soul and *materia prima*: but man is perfected by his rational soul according to the different degrees of perfection, so as to be a body and an animated body and a rational animal. But matter, understood as receiving from the rational soul the perfections of a lower grade—suppose it to be a body and an animated body and an animal —must be understood as suitably disposed for the rational soul that gives the ultimate perfection. Thus the soul, as the form that gives being, has nothing between itself and *materia prima*. Now, since the same form that gives being to matter is also the principle of operation, and because everything acts according to what it actually is, the soul like every other form must be a principle of operation. But we must consider that according to the grades of the forms with respect to the perfection of Being, there is also a grade in their virtue of operating, because that which operates has already an actual existence. Therefore, the more perfect a form is in giving being, the greater is its virtue in operating; and the more perfect forms operate more and with greater diversity than the less perfect. Hence it is that in the less perfect things diversity of accidents is sufficient for diversity of operation, while the more perfect require diversity of parts also, more or less, according to the perfection of the form. Thus we see that fire operates in diverse ways according to the diversity of accidents, such as rising by reason of its lightness, warming by its heat, and so on: yet each of these operations belongs to the fire as a whole. But in animated bodies, which have nobler forms, different parts are assigned for different operations, as in plants the operation of the root is different from that of the boughs or of the trunk; and the more perfect an animated body is, the more does it require, by reason of its greater perfection, a greater diversity in its parts. Therefore, since the rational soul is the most perfect of natural forms, in man do we find the greatest distinction of parts owing to the diversity of his operations; and the soul gives to each of them substantial being in the manner that is suitable to its operations. This is marked by the fact that, when the soul is separated, the flesh or the eye remains only *equivoce*. Now, since the order of instruments must accord with the order of the operations, and, of the diverse operations that are from the soul, one naturally precedes another, so one part of the body must be moved by another to do its own work. Thus then, between the soul as the mover and the principle of operation, and the whole body, there is some medium; for by means of some part first moved it moves the other parts to their work, as by means of the heart it moves the other members to their vital operations. But when it gives being to the body, it immediately gives to every part substantial and specific being. And this is why many people say that the soul, as being the form of the body, is united to the body without a medium, but, as being the mover of the body, is united thereto through a medium: which accords with the opinion of Aristotle, who affirms the soul to be the substantial form of the body. But some people, supposing with Plato that the soul is united

QUALITIES.   67

to the body as one substance to another substance" (that is, one complete substance not resulting therefrom), "had to suppose *media* through which the soul could be united to the body, because diverse and distant substances are not united unless there is something to unite them. And so some of them supposed that a fluid or humour is the medium between the soul and the body, while some supposed it to be light, and others believed it to be the powers of the soul, or something of the sort.* But none of these things are necessary, if the soul is the form of the body. For a thing, whatever it may be, is *one* because it is an *ens*, and therefore, since the form by itself gives being to matter, by itself is it united to *materia prima*, and not by anything else." †

Here ends our long quotation from the Angelic Doctor. It went beyond the question before us by speaking of animated beings and of human beings; but that is not altogether out of place, as we shall see further on.

And now, having discoursed on the mutual operation of the corporeal substances, according to the perfection of their being, we have to see how this can happen between substances far apart. These, as St. Thomas says, must approach

---

* And all they who suppose that the soul is united to the body by means of the biotic fluid, or by ether, or by physical influx, fall into this error.

† *De anima*, art. 9.

in order to operate. "Alteration," he says, "cannot happen without a previous change of place; for in order that the alteration may take place, the alterant must be nearer than before to the altered."* And since this approach may be either by internal attraction or by external impulse, we had better speak of the former as being more difficult.

---
* *Contra Gent.*, iii. 82.

IX.

ATTRACTION.

THAT bodies move towards other bodies, to unite with them, is a fact shown continually by experience. But what is the principle of such movement? It certainly is often extrinsic; and when it is so, its motion is mechanical or forced. But often we find it to be intrinsic, and then the motion is physical or natural, i.e. by true attraction. Now what is this mysterious attraction? How does one body attract another from a distance? Where are the means of (so to speak) pulling it? Are these attracting forces invented for the purpose of hiding our own ignorance?

For the sake of clearness, let us begin with a comparison, and suppose that a cow in a field is attracted by some better grass. The grass, by means of light that makes it visible and the exhalation that carries the scent, is made an *object* for the cow; and the cow, *moved* by its presence, *goes* to it. In this fact we have to distinguish firstly the principle of attraction, which is in the grass: secondly the means by which the attraction is communicated, i.e. light and air: thirdly the manner of attracting, which is by acting on the sensible appetite of the cow through the senses and the imagination: fourthly the principle of motion, by which the cow is moved and *goes;* which is the cow's nature determined actually to go, instead of being merely *in potentia* to do so. But we must remember, that inasmuch as the substantial form or *anima* of the cow is the principle of its every operation, the said nature is its principle of motion in virtue of the substantial form. We must remember also that, in order to be such, it must be endowed with some qualities. For the cow would not go after the grass without having first received an impression from it: nor would the impression suffice without the actual going; nor would the cow actually go, if she had not an antecedent disposition to choose the better grass.

This much is clear in living and sensible creatures: but we may speak analagously of inanimate things also. "We find," says St. Thomas, "a certain operation that in one way is common to the animate and the inanimate things, but in another is proper to the animate, such as motion and generation. For spiritual things absolutely have such a nature that they can move but cannot be moved. Bodies indeed move; but, though one of them can move another, none can move itself; for, as Aristotle proves in

VIII. *Phys.*, those things that move themselves have two parts, of which one is the mover and the other is the moved. But in things purely corporeal this cannot be; for their forms cannot be movers, though they can be a principle of motion by which a thing is moved (UT *quo aliquid movetur*), as, in the motion of the earth, gravity is the principle by which it is moved *(quo movetur)*, but is not the mover." *

To understand this doctrine then we must remember that, if a substance is to move itself, it must have in it two different parts, one the mover and the other the moved. And this is evident, for in that which moves itself there must be the principle and the term of the motion; and if its parts were quite alike, there would be no sufficient reason why the one should be the mover instead of the moved. Hence living things only, as being composed of various parts differently inclined, can move themselves: and this motion within themselves is called an *immanent* action. It is not so with inanimate things. These, not having in their parts any diversity of organism, have no immanent action, but only the action that is called in Latin *transient:* and herein living bodies differ from those without life. Thus we see that, whenever an inanimate body goes to another, it cannot do so by moving itself

---

* *Quæst. Disp.*, *De Veritate*, Q. xxii. a. 3.

as above mentioned, but only by transporting its whole self. The attraction then of inanimate things is in this way: First of all, the body attracted will be disposed for going to one body rather than to another. Secondly, the attracting body must act on the attracted through a medium, and, making itself, so to speak, present to it, become its object. Thirdly, the attracted body must receive an impression (in scholastic language *passio*) sent by virtue of the said medium. Fourthly, having received this, the attracted body must tend actually towards the attractor. And here a question may arise about the attracted body going whole and entire without one part moving the other. To make it clear, we had better begin with an example.

The human soul, being the substantial form of man, does not by one act move the whole body, but, by informing one part, moves another; so that the soul, which informs the whole human body, being the form of a part, is the mover of the other parts. And thus it seems that the motive power originates from the brain and the heart; so that the soul, which informs both, gives by their means movement to the other moveable parts. We may consider the moving part then as a body that gives motion to the contiguous part by transporting its whole self, and thus pressing the part immediately moved by it; for, if we suppose that of the same part one side is the mover and the other the moved, we only remove the question a little, or admit an infinite process repugnant to reason. Here we have the example therefore of a body that in its motion transports its whole self by virtue of the soul, its true substantial form; and therefore it is easy to conceive how a body, even though inorganic, can in virtue of its own substantial form be transported from one place to another.

The Angelic Doctor, speaking of the order and variety of the corporeal universe, finds therein, not a fortuitous collection of many substances, but true dispositions of each for tending mutually to the wondrous formation of the sensible universe.

"All things," he says, "seek a *bonum*, whether they have knowledge or have not. To make this clear, we must know that some ancient philosophers supposed the effects of nature to arise from necessity of preceding causes, and not because the natural causes had a proper disposition for producing such effects. This the Philosopher condemns in the second book of *Physics*, where he shows that, if the relation and mutual utility of things were not in some way intended, they would happen by chance, and therefore would not happen in the greater part, but in the less, like all other things that proceed from chance. We must therefore say that all natural things are ordered and disposed for their proper effects. But a thing may be ordered and directed to another as an end in two ways, viz., either by itself, as when a man directs himself to the place whither he means to go, or by something else, as an arrow is directed to a given place by an archer. Now a thing cannot be directed to an end, unless the director knows the end. For that which directs must have knowledge of that to which it directs; but things that know not the end may be directed to a given end. And this happens in two ways. For sometimes that which is directed to an end is only impelled, without receiving from its director any form to adapt it for this or that direction or inclination; and such inclination is forced, as an arrow aimed at a mark by an archer. But sometimes the directed or inclined thing has from its director or mover some form by which it is adapted for that inclination; and therefore such inclination will be natural, as from a natural principle. Thus He Who gave gravity to stones inclined them to fall naturally downward; and therefore it is said [VIII. *Physics*] that the Maker of heavy and light things is also their Mover. In this way all natural things have an inclination to others that are adapted for them, *having in*

themselves a certain principle of inclination, by reason of which their inclination is natural, so that these in a manner go of themselves, and are not merely led to their proper end *(ita ut quodammodo ipsa vadant, et non solum ducantur in fines debitos.)* But in forced movement things are only led or pushed, not cooperating themselves at all with the mover; but in natural movement things go to their end, inasmuch as they cooperate with the incliner and director by a principle given to them."*
In accordance with this doctrine Dante wrote:

>Ond' ella (Beatrice) appresso d'un pio sospiro
> Gli occhi drizzò ver me con quel sembiante
> Che madre fa sopra figliuol deliro.
>E cominciò : Le cose tutte quante
> Hann' ordine tra loro ; e questo é forma
> Che l'universo a Dio fa simigliante.
>Qui veggion l'alte creature l'orma
> Dell' eterno valore, il quale è fine
> Al quale è fatta la toccata norma.
>Nell' ordine ch' io dico sono *accline*
> Tutte nature, per diverse sorti
> Più al principio loro e men vicine ;
>Onde *si muovono* a diversi porti
> Per lo gran mar dell' essere, e ciascuna
> Con *istinto a lei dato* che la porti.
>
>   *Parad., I.*

What has been said shows clearly the meaning of the triple *appetitus*, so often spoken of by St. Thomas. For, setting aside the forced

---

* *Quaest. Disp., De Veritate*, Q. xxii. a. 1.

motion of things, and considering their natural motion only, we find in the first place that man *petit aliquem terminum* by freely moving himself, because there is in him—that is, in his intellectual knowledge—the known *bonum* that inclines him. Secondly, we find that a brute *petit aliquem terminum*, not freely, and learns by sensitive knowledge the *bonum* that inclines him. Thirdly, we find that an inanimate body, whatever it may be, *petit aliquem terminum*, not by moving itself—because in it there is not a part that moves and a part that is moved—but by an inner principle of motion transporting itself to the term. From this we infer that, as principles of motion, there is a rational appetite in man, a sensitive appetite in brutes, and a natural appetite in substances without life.

"As the sensitive appetite," says St. Thomas, "is distinguished from the natural by its more perfect manner of seeking, so is the rational appetite distinguishable from the sensitive; for the nearer a nature is to God, the more is the Divine dignity expressed in it."

"Now it belongs to the Divine dignity that God should move, incline and direct all things, He being neither moved nor inclined nor directed by anyone. Hence the nearer a nature is to Him, the less is it by Him inclined, and the more is it adapted to incline itself.

Insensible nature, therefore, being, by reason of its materiality, the furthest removed from God, is inclined indeed to some end, but has not in itself anything to incline itself. It has only the principle of inclination, as is evident from what has been said. Now, though a sensitive nature, as being nearer to God, has in itself something that inclines, viz., the *appetibile* apprehended, yet the inclination itself is not in the power of the animal inclined, but is determined from without, (i.e. by God). Animals, when they see a desirable thing, cannot help wishing for it, because they have no dominion over their own inclination. Wherefore they may be said to be drawn, rather than to draw themselves, as St. John Damascene says: which is because the sensible appetitive power has a corporeal organ, and therefore is near to the dispositions of matter and of things corporeal, so as to be moved rather than move. But the rational nature, which is the nearest to God, not only has an inclination to something, as inanimate things have, nor does it only move this inclination by mere extrinsic determination, as sensitive natures do. Over and above that, it has the inclination itself in its own power, so that it does not necessarily incline towards the *appetibile* apprehended, but may either incline or not incline: so that its inclination is not determined for it by another, but by itself.* And this belongs to it not because it uses no corporeal organ, but because, withdrawing from the nature of a moveable thing, it approaches the nature of a mover and operator. Nothing can determine its own inclination to an end without knowing the end and the aptitude of the means to attain it *(habitudinem finis in ea quæ sunt ad finem)*; which reason alone can do. And therefore this appetite, being not determined necessarily by others, follows the apprehension of reason; wherefore the rational appetite, which is called the will, is different from the sensitive appetite." †

From this evidence we gather the noblest conceptions about the wondrous unity of corporeal substances, which in their multiplex tendencies imitate variously the Divine perfections; but we must content ourselves now with noting some deductions that serve our present purpose.

Since the order and beauty of the corporeal universe depends on the reciprocal operations of corporeal substances, and these cannot

---

* Hence whilst human will is evidently determined by God to the universal *bonum*, it is equally clear that the will freely determines itself to the particular objects in which the mind recognizes a participation of that universal *bonum*. And this reconciles the Divine impulse with human freedom as taught by St. Thomas.

† *Quæst. Disp., De Veritate*, Q. xxii. a. 4.

operate without approaching, therefore to all of them an inner inclination is given, called universal gravitation, by which they tend towards each other. As this inclination is solicited (through some medium) by the interchanging action of corporeal substances, so this solicitation receives the name of universal attraction. Thus these substances have a principle by which *(quo)* they attract, and a principle by which they go to the attracting body, and an inner disposition suited for that effect.

But if there were no other than universal gravitation, those substances, though tending by mutual approach to form an aggregate in the universe, would be wanting in that distinction and order from which the beauty of each part results. Moreover the formation of new substances requires that substances should unite and be transformed into other substances of a determinate nature, and that these be disposed for mutual attraction, so as to operate specially on each other. Universal attraction and gravitation would not be sufficient in the universe. Particular attractions and particular gravitations are required, which, though reducible to the same genus, constitute different species. From this chemical affinities arise, and the inclining of certain substances to be united with other determinate substances. Such affinities and inclinations must also have a true cause in the inner disposition of substances, which are therefore said to have affinity to each other, like what we have seen in universal gravitation—like, but not equal, because we cannot speak of species identically, as we speak of a genus. As these dispositions, by the bye, are *qualities*, no wonder if they diminish or fail without a change of the whole substance into another substance. Lastly, it follows, from what we have said, that universal attraction and gravitation being generic and therefore common to all corporeal substances as such, it will outlast their transformation. So that, as the weight of bodies results from gravitation, the weight of the elements will remain in the compound that results, and the weight of the compound will remain in the elements into which it is resolved. Here we must be understood to mean the absolute weight; for we should have to speak otherwise of the specific weight, which is also in proportion to the real volume. Hence, if the specific weight is greater or less in the compound than the absolute weight that was in the elements, greater or less will the absolute weight be; *e converso*. We have now to speak of physical laws, which may be considered as a corollary of the doctrines hitherto explained.

X.

PHYSICAL LAWS.

THIS is a name commonly given: but the conception of it is not always just and distinct, because the philosophers of these days differ much in their doctrine about corporeal natures, and not a few of them, as if in despair of getting at the truth on that point, oscillate between different systems.

Law is a *rule* and *measure* of operations; and law must proceed from reason, because reason alone can properly be a rule and measure. But that alone is not sufficient. Reason must have from Will the power of putting in motion; and therefore Law, which is commanded by Reason, presupposes Will. "Commanding," says St. Thomas, "is an act of reason, presupposing, however, an act of the will."* How the command is expressed he explains thus: "Commanding is essentially an act of reason: for when he who commands orders the commanded to do something, he intimates or threatens."†

---

*1ᵃ. 2ᵃᵉ. Q. xvii. 1.   † Ibid.

Now ordering in the manner of intimation belongs to reason, which can intimate or denounce in two ways. It may intimate in the indicative mood, as when a man says to another, "You ought to do this:" or it may intimate by moving him to do the thing, saying in the imperative mood, "Do this." If it be asked *what* Reason it is that we may call the rule and measure of all created things, unquestionably the answer must be that it is the Divine Reason, which in union with the Divine Will is the rule and exemplar of the whole order of the Universe. The Divine Reason therefore must be considered as universal Law; and as It is Eternal, so must this law be eternal. "Granted that the world is ruled by divine providence," says St. Thomas, . . . "clearly the whole Universe is ruled by Divine Reason:— and therefore that rule of government in God as in the supreme governor of the Universe, has the *ratio* of law. And since the Divine Reason conceives nothing in time, but has an eternal conception, we must therefore say that such law is eternal."* We have, therefore, the eternal divine law which directs with supreme power the order of all created things, that by tending to their different ends they may be the created expression of the Divine goodness, not only in being but also in operating;

---

* *Summa*, 1ª· 2ᵃ· Q. xci. a. 1.

and thus there shines forth in the Universe the image of the Divine perfections, or that extrinsic glory for which the Creator ordered the created universe.

The law, being the rule and measure of the operations, must be applied to those beings that have to operate ; for if it merely remained in the mind of the legislator, it would be to no purpose. "Law," says the Angelic Doctor, "is imposed as a rule and measure. Now the rule and measure is imposed by its application to the things regulated and measured."* This application varies according to the variety of things, which, if rational, participate of the eternal law through the light of reason, which reflecting naturally as a mirror, the very principles of that law, have therefore the proper name of natural law. If they are no more than sensitive, they participate of the eternal law, through the instincts impressed on their nature, which only amount to a knowledge of a term by imagination and a necessary tendency to reach it. If they are without any knowledge at all, they participate of the Eternal Law by means of a disposition in their nature which inclines them to a certain end. "Law, being a rule and measure," says St. Thomas, "may be found in two ways, viz., either in the regulator and measurer or in the regulated or measured.

---

* Ibid. 1ª· 2ᵉ· Q. xc. a. 4.

For that which participates of the law and measure is ruled and measured; and therefore, since all things, being subject to Divine Providence, are regulated and measured by eternal law, as is evident from what has been said (Art. I.), it is evident that all participate somehow of the eternal law, seeing that from the impression of it they have their inclinations to their proper acts and ends. But rational creatures are in a more excellent way under Divine Providence, as being a participant of Providence by providing for themselves and others. Wherefore in them there is participation of the Eternal Reason, through which they have a natural inclination to their proper act and end: and such participation of the eternal law in rational creatures is called natural law. Hence the Psalmist, after saying (Ps. 4), *Sacrificate sacrificium justitiæ*, answers the question, *Quis ostendit nobis bona?* saying, *Signatum est super nos lumen vultus tui, Domine;* as if he had said that the natural light by which we discern what is good from what is bad, which belongs to the natural law, is nothing else than an impression of the Divine light in us. Hence it is evident that the natural law is nothing else than a participation of the Eternal Law in rational creatures." * And speaking of brutes, he

---

* Ibid. Q. xci. a. 2.

remarks, that their participation, not being by the way of reason, cannot properly be called natural law. "Even irrational animals," he says, "participate of the Eternal Reason in their own way; but since rational creatures participate intellectually and rationally, therefore their participation is properly called law, because law is a thing that belongs to reason, as above stated.* But irrational creatures do not participate of it rationally; and therefore it is not called law, except by a similitude." †

And here we must notice particularly what the holy Doctor says about the participation of the Eternal Law in inanimate beings.

"It seems," he objects, "that contingent natural things (i.e., corporeal things without sense) are not under the Eternal Law: for promulgation belongs to law, as was said above: ‡ (but promulgation can only be for rational creatures, to whom something may be announced.) Therefore rational creatures only are under the Eternal Law, and contingent natural things are not under it." But this, he replies, is contrary to what is said in the Book of Proverbs, viii. 29: *Quando circumdabat mari terminum suum, et legem ponebat aquis, ne transirent fines suos.* And he says (in corp. artic.): "We must give one answer about the law of man, and another about the

---

* Ibid., ad 3.   † Ibid., ad 3.   ‡ Q. xc. a.4.

eternal law, which is the law of God; for the law of man does not extend beyond the rational creatures subject to man. The reason of this is, that law is directive of actions adapted to those who are under some one else; so that, properly speaking, no one gives law to his own actions. Whatever things are done about the use of irrational things that are subject to man, are done by the act of the man himself who moves them, because such things do not move themselves, but are moved, as we said.* Therefore man cannot impose a law on irrational creatures, however much they are subject to him, but on rational creatures subject to him he can, inasmuch as by precept or proclamation he impresses on their minds a certain rule which is a principle of action. And as man impresses by proclamation a certain interior principle of action on others who are subject to him, so does God impress on all nature its principles of action *(imprimit toti naturæ principia propriorum actuum)*; and therefore God is said to command all nature; as is said in the Psalms (cxlviii. 6) : *Præceptum posuit, et non præteribit;* and thus every motion and every action of all nature is under the eternal law. Wherefore irrational creatures are under the eternal law in another way" (not as rational creatures are); "for they are

---
* Q. i. a. 2.

moved by Divine Providence, but not through understanding the Divine Precept as rational creatures do." And, in the answer *ad primum*, he says that " the impression of the intrinsic active principle on natural things is like the promulgation of law to man, for through the promulgation of the law a certain directive principle of human action is impressed on men, as was said." (in corp. art.) *

From this we can see clearly what is meant by Physical Laws. For a law may be considered either as in the legislator, who is the measure and rule, or in the things measured and ruled by him. Considered in the legislator, the eternal law, as prescribing the order to be followed by rational creatures in their operations, directing them towards their due proximate ends, and through these to their ultimate end, is called Moral Law. As prescribing the order to be followed by irrational creatures, animate or otherwise, in the operations by which they arrive at certain terms and certain direct ends, it is called Physical Law. Considered in the things measured and ruled, the Eternal Law, *as Moral Law*, is the impress of the Eternal Reason made by mental light on rational creatures, so that in them are the principles of practical truth, as expressions of eternal principles in the Divine Mind: and

---

* Ibid., xciii. a.5.

according to whether those principles are derived from the essence of the things or from the free will of the legislator, that law is called natural or positive. *As Physical Law* it is the impress made by God on all irrational things, that these may tend in their operations to the ends intended by the Eternal Law: and this impress is found in the disposition, instincts and qualities given them by God, by Whose power they are inclined and determined to operate in this or that way rather than in another.

This is what Physical Laws were universally understood to mean; and if the said principles of operation in irrational creatures are to be denied, one fails to see how we can do otherwise than deny the existence of any physical laws, unless we apply the name without any real meaning. As the moral order consists in disposing human actions by the rule of Moral Law existing in human reason, so does the physical order consist in disposing the operations of all irrational creatures by the rule of physical law found in the principles of operation that God communicates to them: and therefore, since moral order cannot be without moral law, neither can physical order be without physical laws. Thus, if we reject the above-stated doctrines, we shall be led by logical necessity either to deny the physical order and harmony manifested in the triple kingdom of nature and in each individual thing therein, or, admitting it, ascribe the same to blind chance, or assert that God is not only the First Supreme and Universal Cause, but also the secondary, immediate and total cause. This last conclusion would involve the risk of falling into the error of those ancient philosophers who said that God is the soul of the Universe; unless, being driven further, we madly affirm, as in fact many do in these days, that God is everything, and everything is God.

And here let us make an end of the general exposition, wherein much will be found wanting as to the various natures of the corporeal universe, their proportions and operations and the many and different phenomena resulting from them. But our purpose is to make evident the constitution of inorganic substances. We have touched on some of their principal and universal properties, now and then speaking of animate creatures, so as to make the rest clearer, and shew the unity and beauty of the system that we call the Physical System. We shall now say why it is called so.

XI.

WHY THE PHYSICAL SYSTEM IS SO CALLED.

WHY (it may be asked) is this system to be called the Physical System, and not the Scholastic System, or the System of Matter and Form?

We cannot call it Scholastic. In the first place that name would not indicate its nature, but only its history; and historically it should rather be called Aristotelian or Peripatetic. Secondly it is well known that, although the Scholastics, generally speaking, agreed about the principal points of philosophy, they differed not a little on other points, especially after Luther had brought into contempt, with the teaching of St. Thomas and Aristotle, not only scholastic Theology but scholastic philosophy also: and Descartes had set himself, by means of a little mechanical motion, to infuse new life into the dead and forgotten system of Epicurus. A man professing himself to be a scholastic may be accused of all the opinions put forth as scholastic of any sort, even in the experimental order, for the purpose of refuting and ridiculing and raising wearisome controversies. Thirdly, some people would carry the dispute from philosophy into history, trying to show that the system here defended was wrongly ascribed to the scholastics. Altogether the name would be unadviseable.

Shall we call it then the system of Matter and Form, or of Materialism and Formalism, as including the Mechanic and Dynamic systems, to each of which belongs one of those names? By no means. The Mechanic System is not strictly a system of Materialism; for that consists in negation of Forms, and has as many degrees as there are degrees of forms. In the first degree form is denied of inanimate substances. In the second it is denied of vegetating things. In the third it is denied of brutes. In the fourth it is denied of man. That system only which admits in all nature nothing more than matter and mechanical motion is *absolute* Materialism: but a very great number of those who profess the Mechanic system are a long way from that, though the passage from one degree to the other is not difficult.

Descartes himself and his most faithful disciples never went beyond the third degree, turning brutes into machines. His recent followers restrict their denial of form to plants, which they take to be machines, and to things without life, which they suppose to consist in a collection of inert atoms. Moreover *materia prima*, as we have shown, is quite different from the said atoms. As to the dynamic system, what have its forces to do with substantial forms ? Those forces are supposed to subsist in mathematical points, whereas substantial forms make corporeal substances, representing, in various ways, the Divine archetypal ideas ; and are not in mathematical points, but in extended matter informed. Since then *materia prima* is not a principle admitted by the Mechanic system, nor is Form admitted by the Dynamic system, consequently the Physical system cannot be the union of the two. Some have said, when treating of the Physical system, that the Physical Sciences, not satisfied with what is given to them by the one or the other of the above mentioned systems, require what is given by both together. But this they said, considering the thing in the abstract and by analogy, not in the concrete and properly : for the physical sciences, demanding a *principle of extension* and a *principle of activity*, are not to be satisfied with inert atoms and mere forces. Therefore the Physical system, as here explained, cannot be called a system of either Materialism or Formalism; but requires a more appropriate name of its own.

" Anyhow," it will be said, " you have no

right to call it Physical. By giving it that name you affirm it to be requisite for the natural sciences commonly called physical, and you exclude all the others invented and defended by philosophers." But we cannot help excluding them. We have shown that Mechanic and Dynamic are names not suitable to the Physical Sciences; and therefore, since all the other systems are reducible to the Mechanic and Dynamic, the system that we are defending has a right to be called the Physical system.

Moreover that name marks the essence of the thing meant, and thus distinguishes it clearly from every other. For the word Φυσικός means *natural:* and the word *nature* means the sum of corporeal substances as having an inner principle of operation. Therefore those inner principles, which the corporeal substances have, are called physical or natural laws. But, as we said before, a corporeal substance is called a nature, because matter is therein united to a substantial form which is its first principle of operation: and therefore the name of "Physical" serves to point out that the system, so called, requires in substances the two-fold principle, material and formal, which constitutes the essence of the same.

"According to the Philosopher," (*V. Metaph.*) says St. Thomas, "the word *nature* was first given to signify the generation of living things, which is called *birth*. And, because such generation is from an intrinsic principle, the name was further understood to mean the inner principle of every motion whatsoever. And so is nature defined in the second Book of Physics. And because this principle is both formal and material, both the matter and the form are commonly called the *nature* of the thing. And because the essence of everything whatsoever is completed by the form, the essence, which is signified by the definition, is commonly called its nature." *

The word Physical then, marks what is proper to the system before us, distinguishing it essentially from every other: and therefore that name is appropriately given to it. In the next chapter we shall have to consider the system relatively.

* P. i. Q. xxix. a. 1 ad 4.

XII.

THE PHYSICAL SYSTEM WITH RESPECT TO PHYSICS IN GENERAL. THE NATURE OF THIS SCIENCE.

IN the division of sciences, whether speculative or practical, we have to consider the proper object of each, not in itself, but as treated by them; and this constitutes the formal object. There are three classes of things that may be the object of speculative science : Firstly, those that are in matter and are considered as in matter; secondly, those that are considered as without matter, but cannot be otherwise than in matter; thirdly, those that transcend matter, either because they cannot be in matter, or because, though they are in matter, they may be separated from it. The first of these three classes gives the object of Physics, for that science deals with sensible things that are in matter and are contemplated as in matter. They are these : 1°. corporeal substances without life ; 2°. those that merely vegetate ; 3°. those that are animate and sensitive, but not rational ; 4°. those that are sensitive, animate and rational. The second class gives us the object of Mathematics, a science that treats of quantity, either continuous, as it is in geometry, or discrete, as in arithmetic and algebra; for although quantity cannot naturally be without matter, nevertheless in those sciences, matter is considered by abstraction as apart from quantity. The third class (i.e., that which transcends matter, etc.) gives us the object of metaphysics, which treat of substances separated from matter, as God and spirits, or of things that may belong to matter, but are also found without it, such as the essence of Being, Substance, *Actus, Potentia*, Cause, effect, &c. Thus the three speculative sciences are Physics, Mathematics, and Metaphysics.

St. Thomas teaches this as follows : " Because," he says, "the first book of Physics, which we purpose to expound, is the first book of natural science, we must first determine what is the matter and the subject of natural science. It must therefore be understood that, since all science is in the intellect, and things become actually intelligible by being in a certain manner abstracted from matter, things belong to different sciences in accordance with their different relations to matter. Again, since every science is acquired through demonstration, and the medium of demonstration is definition, it necessarily follows that sciences differ according to the diversity of their definitions. Be it known then, that there are some things whose being depends on matter, and which without matter cannot be defined. There are others that cannot be except in sensible matter; yet sensible matter does not come into their definition." . . . Of the former sort, he says, are all natural things, as man, for instance, or a stone. Of the latter are all mathematics—as numbers, magnitude, figure. "But there are some things," he goes on to say, "that are independent of matter not only as to their being, but also in our conception of them, either because they never are in matter, as God and other separated substances, or because they are not always in matter, as *substance, potentia, actus* and *Being, (Ens)*. Metaphysics treat of these; mathematics of those that depend on matter for their being, but not in the manner of conceiving them. Natural science, which is called physical, treats of those things that depend on sensible matter both in their being and in the manner of conceiving them. And since all that has matter is moveable, the consequence is that *ens mobile* is the subject of natural philosophy. For natural philosophy treats of natural things: and natural things are those whose principle is nature: and nature is the principle of motion and of rest in that wherein it is. Natural science therefore treats of those things that have in themselves a principle of motion."[*] The holy Doctor requires us to recognize in the object of Physics two properties. The former is that it can neither be nor be defined without matter. The latter (which belongs to the former) is its being endowed with an inner principle of activity or of *nature*. Hence the name of Physics, as we said before.

This will serve to show how vast is the domain of physics, embracing as its proper object every corporeal substance, or, in other words, the whole visible universe. Many, however, give to metaphysics that part which concerns living substances, viz., plants, brutes and man. According to this division, physical science is restricted to things without life, and is called *general* when treating of them as a whole, *special* as discussing the various species; chief among which are chemical physics, mechanical physics and astronomic physics. To go into all these would lengthen our work enormously without serving its purpose: and therefore we restrict ourselves to *General* Physics. Of the others, which are subordinate thereto, we shall show that their fundamental principles are not in opposition to the discoveries of modern science. And here we distinguish between science and scientists: for scientists often disagree among

---
[*] *Comm. Phys. Aris.*, Lib. i. Lect. i.

themselves on many important points, or confine themselves to exposition of facts, setting aside philosophical principles; or explain those facts by hypotheses that fit into their systems but are not grounded on certainty.

XIII.

MECHANICAL INERTIA AND PHYSICAL ACTIVITY OF BODIES.

IN its primary signification *inertia* means want of art, and in that sense a thing that operates without art would be called inert. But afterwards it was extended to mean inactivity or even laziness. *Lustremus animo has artes*, says Cicero, *quibus qui carebant inertes nominabantur. Postea tamen consuetudo obtinuit, ut pro ignavo potius et deside accipiatur.** Lastly it was employed to mean the want of an inner principle of activity. And in this sense bodies are called inert. The question of whether they are so, or not, is differently solved, and, according to the solution of it, men philosophize variously about corporeal things.

The followers of the Mechanic system say that bodies have no principle of physical activity, and reduce all natural phenomena to shocks mutually given and received by atoms. Hence their principle: "There is nothing in

---
* III. *de Fin.*

nature but matter and motion: and motion proceeds from motion alone." Some of the Dynamic school come near to this opinion: which at first sight seems very strange and contradictory. But they soften it off in a way, assigning to all corporeal beings not an intrinsic, but an extrinsic inertness: and so they say that forces *per se* subsisting can operate on themselves, but not reciprocally, because they are distant from each other. Hence they fall back on pre-established harmony or occasionalism, laying down that two forces show a mutual operation because they are inly determined by God to operate, or because God alone operates in both. Others admit action *in distans* and reciprocal activity of forces. All these hypotheses are in contradiction to the Physical system.

The Physical system acknowledges mechanical inertness, as common to all corporeal substances without life, and physical activity as common to them all in different ways. And in the first place, when we speak of mechanical *inertia*, we must understand it to mean that a body is capable of passing, by extrinsic impulse, from rest into motion, and incapable of changing by itself either the direction or the velocity of the motion. Both reason and experience will show that bodies are of themselves moveable, not requiring to occupy this or that portion of space more than another, and therefore that, when there is space and a cause able to give a suitable impulse, there is no sufficient reason why a body should not leave the place where it was. If the body is an atom, it cannot operate on itself, because *immanent* action is not proper to it, but only *transient* action, inasmuch as it acts on other bodies, but not on itself. Not operating on itself, it cannot free itself, so to speak, from the impulse received, nor increase it, nor change its direction. Reason then demonstrates mechanical inertia : and experience is continually proving that, when there are no impediments nor attraction and no repulsion of other bodies, an inanimate body goes by the impulse received, without ever changing its direction or otherwise modifying its motion.

But if bodies are mechanically inert, they are not physically so. Why, as the Angelic Doctor says, may we not allow all created substances to have a true physical efficiency and causality ? To suppose that we may not would never occur to anyone capable of contemplating God's Infinite Goodness. The creative *fiat* brought all things out of nothing, and God saw that they were *good*, as participating of His own Goodness. Now the Divine Goodness not only requires perfection of being, but tends also to diffuse itself, because *bonum est diffusivum sui*. Therefore, since God created all things good, He imparts to them not only Being, but also that property of Good which consists in diffusing itself by operation. Like St. Dionysius and St. Augustine, the holy Doctor teaches that the Divine Goodness was the Cause of all things. "For God willed," said St. Thomas, "to communicate to creatures, as much as possible, the perfection of His goodness. Now the Divine Goodness has a twofold perfection: firstly, in respect of Himself as eminently containing every perfection; secondly, in respect of His operating on things, inasmuch as He is their Cause. Wherefore, it accorded with the Divine Goodness that this double perfection should be communicated to creatures, so that every created thing should, by the Divine Goodness, be made not only to be good, but also to give being and goodness to others, as the sun by diffusion of its rays makes bodies not only illuminated but luminous."*

He remarks moreover that the faculty of operating is a natural consequence of being; so that whenever God gives being to a thing, He must enable it naturally to be a cause by its own operation. "That which gives the principal thing to something," says St. Thomas,

---

* *Quæst. Disp., Q. de Veritate*, V. De Prov. 8.

"gives to the same all things that are a consequence of it. . . . Now doing *in actu* is a consequence of being *in actu*; as is evident in God, Who is the *Actus Purus* and the first Cause of the being of all things. . . . If therefore He communicated His likeness to things by making them be, it follows that He communicated His likeness to them by enabling them to act, so that each creature should have its proper operation."*

And the holy Doctor shows that, if the true efficiency of creatures be denied, the order of the universe, with its beauty and perfection, disappears. "To take away order from created things," he says, "is to take away what is best in them; for the individual things are good in themselves; but all of them together are best because of the order of the Universe; for the whole is always better than the parts, and is the end for which they are. But if their power of acting be taken away, the mutual interchanging order of things is taken away also. In fact things different in their natures cannot be bound together in the unity of order unless some are acting and others acted upon. It is therefore wrong to say that things have not their proper operations."† Passing over many other reasons which he brings forward to prove a true efficiency in all

---

* *Contra Gent.*, iii. 69. † Ibid.

corporeal substances, we need only quote what he says in another part of the same chapter at the conclusion of an argument: "To deny, therefore," he says, "that created things have their proper operations, is to derogate from the Divine Goodness." *

But why should we look for philosophical arguments, when all nature speaks to us, persuades us, compels us to confess the truth about this? If we raise our eyes towards Heaven, we find it in the gravitation of the heavenly bodies and the marvellous laws of their revolutions. If we look on the earth, we have it in the fertilization of seeds, the formation of embryos, the increase of all living beings, the transformation of elements into compounds. If you acknowledge true activity, you can find your way in the labyrinth of your researches about light, heat, electricity, magnetism. Deny it, and you have to grope about without any guide at all. With the doctrine that acknowledges the efficiency of all secondary causes, that vary more or less by the rule of their comparative perfection, the whole universe becomes one harmonious chorus that sings the glories of its Maker. The contrary doctrine makes the universe mute. All is mystery—not such a mystery as raises and sublimates the intellect of the believer,

---
* Ibid.

but a mystery that abases, depresses, destroys.

We need not give other proofs here of such physical activity and efficiency in each of the substances. We shall only remark that, in this its fundamental doctrine, the Physical system agrees completely with the teaching of the Catholic Church. The greatest theologians have not hesitated to affirm that we cannot deny it without incurring the taint of rashness. "We must say," writes the great Suarez, "that created agents work, truly and properly, effects connatural and proportional to themselves. And I believe that this truth is not only most evident to sense and reason, but also most certain according to Catholic doctrine. Therefore, as for the former reason, St. Thomas called the contrary opinion foolish, so for the latter reason we may call it rash and erroneous, and, as such, deservedly rejected by all philosophers and theologians. . . Not immaterial substances only, but also material substances have a physical and true efficiency. This follows from the preceding doctrine with almost equal demonstration and certainty; for experience, reason and evidence speak as strongly in favour of natural and material causes as of immaterial causes."* And Ruvio says plainly that: *Tollere efficientiam ab omnibus causis, vel etiam corporeis, error est non solum*

---

* *Met. Disp.*, 18, Sect. 1.

in fide catholica, sed in vera philosophia. *
Cardinal Toledo speaks in like manner: *Auferre efficientiam,* he says, *ab iis causis particularibus, nec est sacræ doctrinæ, nec doctoribus sanctis, nec veræ philosophiæ consonum.* † We are not bringing a theological doctrine to bear on our contradictors, for that in a philosophical treatise would not be allowable. But we have a right to say that those who would not reason on created things under the guidance of true philosophy destroyed science, and substituting their own wild imaginings, incurred the danger of that punishment with which God Himself has threatened them: *Quoniam non intellexerunt opera Domini, et in opera manuum ejus, destrues illos, et non ædificabis eos.* ‡

---

* *In II. Phys.*, Tract. 2, Q. 2.   † *In II. Phys.*, 3.   ‡ *Ps.* xxvii. 5

XIV.

OBJECTIONS AGAINST THE DOCTRINE PROPOSED.

DIFFICULTIES direct and indirect are put forward against the true physical activity of bodies. The indirect difficulties are put forward by the followers of the Mechanical system, in a vague and abstract manner, to support their own opinion: and these we have sufficiently refuted. We shall now answer the direct arguments against the doctrine itself, and begin by quoting from Malebranche.

"If," he says, "anyone supposes that there are in bodies entities distinct from matter, and has not a distinct idea of matter, he will easily be led to imagine that these bodies are the true and chief causes of those effects which are seen to happen. Nay, that is the opinion of ordinary philosophers, who, to explain these effects, argue that there are substantial forms, real qualities and other like entities. But if we set ourselves to consider the idea of the cause or the power of operating, we cannot doubt that it represents a something divine. For the idea of a sovereign power is the idea of a sovereign divinity, and the idea of a subject power is the idea of an inferior divinity, but still a true divinity, at least according to the judgment of the pagans, always supposing it to be the idea of a true power or a true cause. One admits then, something divine in all the bodies around us, when one admits forms, faculties, qualities, virtues, or real beings capable of producing certain effects by force of their nature; and thus, one is insensibly brought into agreement with the pagans, by reason of respecting their philosophy. True it is that faith recalls us to our duty : but perhaps it may be rightly said that in this, if the heart is Christian, the mind is fundamentally pagan. . . .

" Moreover it is difficult to persuade ourselves that we ought neither to fear nor love true forces, beings that have the faculty of operating on us, of punishing us by pain and rewarding us by pleasure. And since true adoration is in love and fear, it furthermore becomes difficult to persuade ourselves that we ought not to adore them. . . . The feeling that we ought to love or fear where there is a true cause of good or evil, seems to be so natural and just, that on no account ought we to throw it off. Therefore, given that false philosophical opinion which we are endeavouring to destroy, viz., that the bodies around us are true causes of the good and evil experienced by us, reason would seem to justify a religion like that of the pagans, and approve of universal dissoluteness of manners. It is true that reason teaches us not to adore leeks and onions, for instance, as the Supreme Divinity, because we are not made completely happy by having them, nor completely unhappy by not having them; and therefore the pagans never rendered the same honour to them as to the Supreme Jove, on whom all this divinity depended. . . . But though we should not be justified in rendering supreme honour to leeks and onions, we may always give to them some particular adoration. I mean that we may have a regard for them, and somehow love them, if it is true that somehow they can do us good, in proportion to which they should be honoured."* Alarmed at the sight of so frightful a precipice, he uttered a cry of warning to the scholastics, and, imploring them to have pity on themselves, proposed, as the only means of escape and security, his Mechanical system.

Were his accusations true, we should have to shed bitter tears over the memory not only of Aristotle and Plato, but also of St. Augustine and the other Fathers and Doctors of the

---

* *Rech. de la Ver.*, I. vi. p. ii.

Church, who would, all of them, have been deluded by pagan philosophy, and have, all of them, taught idolatry.

Strange it is that Malebranche should have made those charges against experience of facts, against reason, against the authority of so many great men, illustrious by their wisdom as by their holiness, and strangely too, (considering that he was a Catholic) against the teaching of the Catholic schools, which the Church, as the greatest theologians testify, has so approved as to make it her own. What can we say about him? Certain it is that, owing to his antipathy to matter and form, he looked upon everything else as unimportant, and spoke like a madman; so that answering him is a sheer waste of time.

Our acknowledging a principle of physical activity in corporeal substances will not make us idolaters, as long as we admire in the creatures endowed with it the goodness of God, Who gave and preserves their Being and their power of operating, and cooperates with the operator. There is no danger of our falling into idolatry while, by the order, beauty, variety and magnificence of those things, and by all that strictly proceeds from their activity, our minds are raised up to the infinite perfection of the Cause Who produced them and made them operate. You would never dream of saying that because the sun's rays are not the sun, they are not bright. Rather would their beauty invite you to contemplate that ocean of light from which they come.

But the sun diffuses its rays by necessity of nature, whereas God, of His own most free and bounteous Will, imparts a likeness of Himself to the secondary causes, that operate according to that Will. Of His pure goodness, as the Angelic Doctor says, He, Who has no need of anything, (because His perfection does not depend on anything external,) has communicated to other beings also the dignity of being a cause. As to the only proof put forward by Malebranche in support of his charges, viz., that if created substances operated physically, they would do good or harm to us and be worthy of love, in which the adoration due exclusively to God consists, our answer is that it proves nothing, unless we wish to maintain that loving parents, relations and friends is giving them divine adoration. What he meant by saying that, if we believe in substantial forms and therefore in physical activity, we might love leeks and onions, we cannot understand. He ought to have known that love, as here understood, is a rational, not a sensitive affection, and therefore is only for those who have the dignity of a person, which irrational creatures have not.

Modern teachers bring forward another objection, by which many are deceived. "Who," they say, "can form a conception of this form, this principle of physical activity? Is it a body or a soul? You will not allow it to be a body, therefore it must be a soul: and thus the world would be populated with souls, as many souls as there are atoms." This objection, though obtruded on us now, is of an earlier date, having been used by more than one Cartesian as a valid argument against scholastic philosophy. Descartes, as is well known, laid down a criterion of truth, viz.: "That which is contained in a clear and distinct idea is true." From which we pass on quickly to this other: "That which is not a clear and distinct idea is false." But this, if admitted with all its consequences, is as destructive to faith as to science. Destructive it is to faith; for we should have to reject as lies all the mysteries of faith, because we cannot have a clear and distinct idea of them. Of its being destructive to science we have a proof before us. They began by asking what these forms and principles of activity are. We cannot have a clear and distinct idea of them; and therefore according to them, they do not exist. We cannot have a clear and distinct idea of one principle of life in plants: and therefore plants are a clashing

H

together of inert atoms. But we cannot have a clear and distinct idea of the *anima* of brutes, which is neither a spirit nor a body. Therefore they are machines artificially put together, and all their movements are mechanical. And what can we say about the union of the human soul with the body? However much we may try, we cannot succeed in forming a clear and distinct idea of that. We must therefore say that the human soul is only present to the body, or at most directs it, like the engine-driver of a locomotive, without communicating to it any true force. And who can form a clear and distinct idea of the human soul itself, as a spirit quite without form and figure? We should have to say that it is the phosphorus of the brain, and that its movements are our acts of reasoning and will. And how can we have a clear and distinct idea of the origin of things, of their mutual action, of the order and the laws to which they are subject? It is much more convenient to get rid of the difficulty by reducing all this to human ways of thinking. And then, who can venture to say that he has a clear and distinct idea of God—a Being spiritual and immense, free and immutable, most simple and infinite? It is easier to acknowledge no God other than the world itself, and leave the world without God.

What else? The very idea of Being is then so thickly veiled, that its essence, modes, origin and properties become impenetrable: and yet Being cannot be altogether denied. And so we come to universal doubt, as the first step in philosophical discovery, or rather to Hegel's principle that Being is Non-Being; which crowns the edifice, and has the one good effect of making it no longer possible for the opponents of the old philosophy to understand each other.

We cannot, in fairness, be expected to say anything in reply to men who stigmatize as false everything of which, by reason of not ascending from effects to causes, from operations to operators, they cannot in their own mind form a clear and distinct idea. As to the particular difficulty alleged, it is a curious thing to hear people repeat that we cannot possibly have a clear idea of physical activity, of substantial forms, of attraction, and therefore that all this must be voted to be a chimera (or, as some say, *fictitious, abstract beings*, or *realized abstractions*); when for so many centuries the brightest geniuses have attested the contrary, and even now, so many noble thinkers find therein the foundation of that one philosophy which, besides being the handmaid of theology, can be fruitfully applied to explaining the phenomena of nature. What shall we say in particular to the followers of the Dynamic system, who cry up the clearness of their forces, which are qualities without a subject? Or what shall we say to the Mechanic school with its inert atoms, from whose incomprehensible whirlings come forth wholly and in its parts, the nature, order and beauty of the Universe?

The general objections brought against the forms and physical activity of substances are reducible to the two above mentioned. Of the special objections to this or that mode of activity we shall treat in their proper places, when we come to speak of the various forms under which that activity shows itself.

XV.

ACTION AT AN ABSOLUTE DISTANCE.

IT is a fixed principle in St. Thomas's physical system that the agent and the patient must be conjoined, and therefore that action at an absolute distance is impossible and absurd: but the agent may be substantially distant from the patient, if the two are conjoined by virtue of a medium. The Scholastics, therefore, said that the *immediatio suppositi* is not always necessary, the *immediatio virtutis* being sufficient in finite causes. "However great the virtue of the agent may be," says St. Thomas, "it cannot act on anything distant, except through a medium,"* and because the virtue of God is not really distinguishable from His essence, the holy Doctor adds that, "To act immediately on all things belongs to the most great virtue of God. Wherefore nothing is so distant that God is not in it." And he exemplifies this with regard to finite agents by saying that he who operates, being absent, is not the proximate cause of the thing

---
* *Summa*, P. i. Q. viii. 1 ad 3.

done, but its remote cause, as the sun's virtue is first impressed on a body conjoined to it, and so on successively; which virtue, as Avicenna says, is its light, by which it acts on inferior things. There is more sense in this than in the sayings of modern scientists, who talk about ethereal atoms very far apart, and oscillations of light parallel to each other, so that the ethereal atoms never can meet; while the sun nevertheless communicates its virtue by atomic ethereal motion to all things, and by illuminating, fructifies them.

When we consider the facts of nature, we always find valid arguments for a general induction that created causes never operate at a distance: and philosophical reasoning makes us draw the same conclusion. For if we admit that a substance can operate on another, in spite of an absolute void between, we must admit an effect without a cause. In fact, if there are two substances, A and V, separated by an absolute void, and A is to operate a change, X, on V, between these there must be a virtue, a force, a cause, productive of that change. Now this virtue and the substance whence it proceeds are either conjoined or not conjoined. If they are conjoined, A must be in true contact with V, and that upsets the hypothesis of absolute distance. If they are not conjoined, that virtue must either depend on another substance, to which it was transmitted from A, or it must subsist of itself. In the former case the hypothesis of action absolutely at a distance would vanish: in the second we should be affirming what is contrary to nature. Substance alone can subsist of itself. Every virtue or force or quality or accident must be inherent in a substance as in its proper subject. Therefore that virtue or force of A cannot detach itself and fly alone to V; but, in order to arrive there, must be consigned, so to speak, first to B, then from B to C, and from C to D, and from D to E, and so on, through a series of intermediate substances, till it comes to that which is in immediate contact with V, like the mechanical movement communicated from the first to the last in a series of balls apart from each other. Hence the Scholastic principle, that the operator and the thing operated on must be conjoined, either *immediatione suppositi* or *immediatione virtutis*.

The illustrious Cardinal Toledo says in his Commentaries on Aristotle: " Substance that moves anything or is the cause of some change therein, is twofold, viz., either mediate and remote, or immediate and proximate. It is immediate when there is no mover between it and the thing that it moves, as fire burns the wood to which it is conjoined. It is mediate when between it and the thing that it moves there is some other substance, as fire warms distant objects through the medium of air. . . . Moreover, when any substance operates between, and thereby produces an effect at a distance, *that effect is not always the same in the medium and in the distant object.* Fire, through the medium of glass, liquifies wax, not the glass: and the reason is, that one and the same accident received in various subjects produces in them different effects according to their various dispositions; and thus heat makes one subject white, another black. . . . Therefore, though the same accident be received in the medium and in the remote object, the effect in them is not always equal. . . ." Hence we may lay down this first conclusion, that if there is not some immediate mover, no true change can take place. This is an axiom of the Peripatetics. In fact it is inconceivable that one substance could produce a change in another without it, either immediately or through the medium of something else: for the operation and the being are conjoined, and therefore where a substance is not, its operation will not be. Thus, when a substance does not operate on another at a distance by communicating its own operation to a medium, it cannot by any means be found operating in that substance.

Hence theologians validly argue that God is present everywhere, precisely because He operates everywhere. . . . And now let us lay down a second conclusion, that the proximate mover and the moved are always together, and immediately together. For though the former is far off in its *suppositum*, its virtue is always immediate. And thus we must understand Aristotle to mean that no change, of any sort, can take place unless the mover and the moved are together. We must not suppose him to have believed that all the movers are contemporaneous."*

The Conimbrican † commentators of the Stagirite furnish us with another argument on the question, and one that is not to be despised. Every substance, they say, has a sphere of action, beyond which it cannot produce any sensible effect: but if it could operate from an absolute distance, it could also extend its virtue to any degree of remoteness. Therefore, operating at a truly absolute distance cannot be admitted. The minor proposition is certain: for supposing an operation at an absolute distance, the more or less of distance gives no reason for limiting the extent of the operating power. The precise words of the authors are as follows: " If a thing can, without a medium, operate on another at a distance,

---

* *In VII. Phys.*, Q. 2.   † Coimbrian, antico Conimbrican.

philosophers have no reason to say that every agent has its determined sphere of action: for the agent could not diffuse its action to *any given* distance, if its virtue did not pass through a medium in which it is gradually spent and weakened." *

It is not worth while to put forward other reasons. Common sense tells us that, as nothing can act before it exists, no cause can operate in a place where as yet it is not in any way, either by itself *(immediatione suppositi)* or by its virtue *(immediatione virtutis)*: for that would imply an effect without a cause.

It will not be amiss to speak of some doctrines that were affirmed and are affirmed even now. Firstly then, it is false that the agent A can operate an effect on V without communicating its whole virtue to the medium between, but only causing some change in the substance immediate to itself. This is evidently false, because in that case there would be, for a moment at least, action truly at a distance. Secondly, it is false that any medium whatsoever is sufficient between A and V, for the one to operate on the other. Not every substance is adapted to receive in the same way the qualities of another. We can see this in bodies that transmit badly either light or heat or electricity or magnetic

---
* *In VII. Phys.*, Q. i, a. 2.

virtue, and therefore are called bad conductors. For if a medium is necessary to transport the action of A into V, an insufficient medium would mean action truly at a distance. Hence it follows, thirdly, that merely operating on V, anyhow, would not be sufficient. A must operate in a manner adapted for transmitting its action into V: for the change in V would equally be an effect without a cause, whether we supposed it to proceed from A without a medium, or whether we supposed it to be caused by A with a medium, but without communicating anything proportionate to that change. Thus we find that many substances conduct certain operations of other substances well, others badly, as in the phenomena of light, heat, electricity and magnetism.

It is puerile to say that the absolute distance between the agent and the patient is too small to be worth considering: for action at an absolute distance is essentially repugnant to reason. The more and the less have no place in what concerns the essence of things.

This alone would show the falseness of the Mechanic and Dynamic systems, that oppose the Physical system: for they who profess them cannot avoid admitting action at a distance.

With this criterion we can also refute certain modern doctrines that find support from the science of the day, such as modern magnetism and hypnotism: for the very singular phenomena put forward in support of these doctrines are attributed by some people not to good spirits, because that would be repugnant to the holiness of such, nor to evil spirits, lest consciences should be disturbed, but to the operations of nature. Now, in the first place, the human soul with its intellect and will cannot immediately join itself to the intellect and will of other human beings, nor to any external bodily thing. Secondly, to enter into communication with other men, it must compose sensible signs of its own acts, as, for instance, words or other external signs, and then the other people to whom the signs are directed, must have previously known the value of them: for otherwise they might feel the impressions, but would not understand the meaning of them. Moreover we should require some suitable medium for sending to others the signs of our thoughts and wishes; for otherwise we should have recourse to *actio in distans*, which we have shown to be absurd. To fall back on our ignorance about the reach of physical forces is not reasonable: and still less is it philosophical. True it is that we often do not know the value of those forces: but we certainly do know that they never can make an absurdity, and that it is an absurdity to suppose action at a distance, however small,—as above shown.

XVI.

MOTION.

IN general all change whatsoever is motion. One Being only is in rest. That Being is God, Who is immutable. All created things may be said to be more or less in a state of change and motion, especially corporeal things, whose nature and operations have to be considered by the physical philosopher. Let us begin therefore by giving Aristotle's definition of motion: "Motion is the act of Being that is *in potentia* as such."

This at first sight may seem somewhat obscure, especially to anyone who, having accustomed himself to be satisfied with descriptive and superficial definitions, cares little or nothing for those that penetrate and explain the essence of things. But let us see what St. Thomas says about it in his commentary on Aristotle's *Physics*. "We must know," he says, "that some have defined motion as the non-instantaneous coming forth of the actual from the potential: but this definition is erroneous, because they put into it that which presupposes motion.

Coming forth is a species of motion: and the word *instantaneous* regards time, instantaneous being that which happens in an indivisible point of time, and time being defined by motion. Hence it is impossible to define motion by previous notions better known *(per priora et notiora)*, except as the Philosopher defines it. For, as we have said, everything is divided into the potential and the actual. But *potentia* and *actus*, being among the first differences of being, are naturally prior to motion: and the Philosopher uses them in defining motion. We must consider therefore that some things are actual only, and others potential only, and others midway between the potential and the actual. Now that which is *in potentia* is not yet moved. That which already is *in actu perfecto* is not moved, but has been moved. That which is being moved is midway between the potential and the actual, being partly *in potentia* and partly *in actu*: and this is evident in alteration. For water, when hot *in potentia* only, is not yet moved or changed. When already hot, the movement of heating is ended. But if it participate of heat imperfectly, it is then moving towards being hot; for that which is becoming hot participates of heat gradually by little and little. Therefore that imperfect act of heat in the thing that is being heated is motion, not as actual only, but inasmuch as, being an act, it has a disposition for a further act, because, if that disposition were taken away, the act, however imperfect, would terminate the motion, instead of being motion, as when anything is incompletely heated. But the disposition for a further act belongs to what is potentially that further act. In like manner, if the imperfect act be considered merely in order to the further act, according to which it means a *potentia*, it has not the essence of motion, but of a principle of motion, for heating may begin from what is tepid, as well as from what is cold. Thus therefore the imperfect act has the essence of motion, as a *potentia*, in comparison with an ulterior act, and as an act, in comparison with something more imperfect. Wherefore motion is neither the *potentia* of that which is potentially, nor the act of that which is actually. It is the act of what is *in potentia*, the word *act* referring to an anterior *potentia*, and the word *potentia* referring to an ulterior act. Most suitably therefore did Aristotle define motion to be the ἐντελέχεια, i.e. the act of Being existing *in potentia*, as such: *Motus est actus existentis in potentia secundum quod hujusmodi.* *

Evidently this definition of motion is general, defining the genus, not the species. So

---

* St. Thomas, *III. Physic.*, Lect. 2.

considered, motion requires two terms, and, like a tide, ebbs and flows between them. One term is the *terminus a quo*, and is the principle of motion. The other is the *terminus ad quem*, and is the end of motion, viz., rest. The thing in motion cannot have reached the *terminus ad quem*, or it would be at rest; nor can it be in the *terminus a quo*, or it would not yet be in motion. It must be between the one and the other, leaving the former and tending towards the latter. Every change is precisely the transit from the one term to the other. In the former case the thing may change. In the latter it has changed. Between them it is changing: and precisely between these two every change is motion. Therefore God, Who is the most perfect and immutable Act, has no perfection potentially, cannot pass from not possessing to possessing, so as to rest in a *terminus ad quem*. Hence in God all motion whatsoever is impossible. But in all creatures there is, firstly, *potentia*, secondly, an imperfect act, lastly, a complete act: and therefore that between the two terms *a quo* and *ad quem*, has the true essence of motion. Hence in the created intellect, in the will, in the sensitive and vegetative faculties, and in every alteration, there is the generic essence of motion: but in each of these the specific essence evidently varies. And since all creatures, by the necessity of their contingent being, are *in potentia*—therefore are imperfect and perfectible—so in them there is essentially the principle of motion, which, as was said elsewhere, is called nature.

Hence, as St. Thomas remarks with Aristotle, he who has not a true knowledge of what motion is can never have a true notion of nature, and therefore cannot reason rightly about natural things. *Natura*, he says, *est principium motus. . . . Et sic patet quod, ignorato motu, ignoratur natura, quum in ejus definitione ponatur. Quum ergo nos intendamus tradere scientiam de natura, necesse est notificare motum.* * And here we cannot help noticing, by the way, the wisdom with which in that philosophy the First Cause, the First Mover, Almighty God, was called the Immoveable Being, and all created beings were called moveable. The Essence of God is incompatible with motion. The essence of created beings is, of its own necessity, ordered for motion. Hence, the word *nature* is, in its proper sense, applicable to created essences, but to the Divine Essence in an analogical sense only.

With regard to the species of motion we may remark firstly that motion, if it means the quality, is called alteration ; but if it means the quantity, it is called increase or decrease.

---
* *Ibid. In III. Phys.* Lect. 1.

Thus through a change of quality a liquid is altered, or an animal through illness, while a plant or animal has a movement of increase if growing, or contrariwise of decrease. Local movement, i.e. the passing of a corporeal substance from one place to another, is called translocation, or change of place.

Here it must be remarked that in physics we have to consider the motion of material beings only. In them the motion, whatever it may be, is generically different from what it is in immaterial beings, as the angels are, and human souls when separated from the bodies which they had informed. In such immaterial beings motion is a non-material change.

And now let us go a little further in considering the said motion of physical things. The first of all motions in order of time is local motion, because the others presuppose it, as the Angelic Doctor, in accordance with Aristotle, tells us in these words:

"He (Aristotle) begins by laying down what he means to show: and he says that, of the three species of motion—one according to quantity, which is called increase and decrease, another according to quality, which is called alteration, and another according to place, which is called change of place—the last-named must be the first of all. And secondly, he proves this by the fact of its being impossible that increase can be the first of motions, because it cannot take place without a previous alteration. For that by which anything is increased is in a way similar and in another way dissimilar. It is evidently dissimilar: for that by which anything is increased is nourishment, which at first is different from what it nourishes; but when it does nourish, it must be similar. Now it cannot pass from dissimilarity to similarity without alteration. Increase, therefore, must be preceded by alteration, through which the nourishment passes from one disposition into another. Thirdly, he shows that every alteration is preceded by local motion. When anything is altered, there must be something that alters it, making (for instance) actually hot that which before was potentially so. But if that which causes the alteration were always equally near to the altered thing, it would not cause the heat now rather than sooner. Evidently therefore the mover of the alteration is not always at the same distance from that which is altered, but sometimes nearer and sometimes further. This cannot happen without change of place." *

A little further on the holy Doctor speaks of the generation of substances. Without quoting the passage, it will suffice to say that

---
* *Ibid. In VIII. Phys.* Lect. 14.

generation cannot happen without the alteration and concurrence of the generators where it should take place. Now all this supposes local motion: and therefore local motion precedes every other motion of corporeal substances.

And now, to examine from a more philosophic and important point of view the doctrine explained, let us consider how some created causes are immaterial and others material. An immaterial cause is a cause that does not in its own being and operation depend on matter; so that matter does not co-operate in the operation as a principle, though it may do so as a term.

Every angel (to say nothing of God) is a cause that can operate on corporeal and material beings; but matter does not co-operate at all therein as a principle of the operation. Hence an angel may in substance and by operation be where a corporeal substance is, and operate on it, and operate at the same time at which the corporeal substance operates: but it cannot constitute therewith one principle of operation. This is philosophically expressed by the saying, that an angel can be the *forma assistens* of a body, but not its *forma informans*. A material cause is that which in its being and operation so depends on matter, that matter is a co-principle of operation; as for instance, the principle of activity in any elementary atom, or the vital principle of plants, or the sensitive principle of brutes. These principles cannot of themselves either be or operate: and therefore, to sustain them, they require a subject with which they can operate as a co-principle. Hence the adequate subject of the operations of things inanimate, of plants, and of brutes, is not the principle of activity alone, nor the substantial form only, but, more correctly, the form and the matter together. Therefore these principles and their relative powers are called organic. Now man is the link that unites in himself this twofold causality, material and immaterial; for his spiritual soul is the substantial form of matter, as the *anima* of the brute is. As being spiritual, it has powers or faculties and operations that are proper to itself and inorganic. Such are the faculties of understanding and of willing. As the substantial form of matter, it has powers or faculties and operations that depend on matter, as those of a brute do. Hence the essential difference between the vegetative or the sensitive powers and those that are intellective lies in this: that the latter are inorganic, and the former organic.

If then the being and operating of an immaterial cause is without matter, it cannot when operating, admit *in itself* local motion, though able to effect it at the term of action: whereas, contrariwise, a material cause always operates with local motion. Hence every operation of organic things, of plants, or of brutes, is done with such local motion.

But then in man we must distinguish the operations. Those that proceed from spiritual or inorganic faculties are not done with local motion: but those that proceed from organic faculties, such as the acts of vegetative life, of animal appetites and of imagination, &c., are done with local motion. And since, as philosophy shows, the acts of the spiritual or inorganic faculties presuppose or draw with them those of the material faculties, therefore in man every act of the former is succeeded by a true local motion through the operating of the latter: and evidently this motion, wherever it may take place, will vary according to the variation of the powers and acts by which it is produced. Thus, for instance, it will be different in the imaginative power and in the imagination from what it is in the animal *appetitiva* and its tendencies; different again in the faculty of sight and the act of seeing; different in the faculty of hearing and the act of hearing; different in the *vegetativa* and the act of assimilating; and so on, in every operation derived from material power.

It must therefore be maintained, firstly,

that a material or corporeal substance operates with local motion : secondly, that such motion will vary according to the operation. Thirdly, therefore, the motion will be immanent where the operation is immanent, i.e. one that has its proper term within the same individual, as it does in living things. Fourthly, it will be transient *(transiens)* * where the operation is so, as it is in living things and in things without life, when the substance, that is the cause, operates outside itself. Fifthly, every passion or modification in a material substance that receives the action of another will be done with local motion, which local motion will vary according to the passion or modification.

Anyone who will think a little about these things will easily see how far from the truth are those who, not caring to penetrate to the diversity of essence and of operations in immaterial and material causes, confuse the operations of the latter with local motion, because they always find it accompanied by local motion. They conclude therefore that " in

---

* I.e. in the sense of going beyond itself. How can one translate *transiens* into the anti-philosophic language of Protestant England, where "immaterial" is understood to mean unimportant, "formal" to mean absurdly ceremonious, and the two are marvellously jumbled in "a matter of form"? "Transient" is supposed to mean something not permanent, and "transitive" is applied to nothing but verbs. Will any good Christian oblige me with a valid translation of the word ?—*Trans.*

nature there is only local motion," on the principle that *hoc est cum illo, ergo est hoc*. This is giving all to the senses and nothing to the intellect. By rule of reasoning our conclusion can only be this: If in all the operations of corporeal substances we find, as in fact we do, a true local motion, various according to their variations, we have no right to infer therefrom that in nature there is nothing but matter and motion—thus excluding every principle of physical activity that causes motion—but only that the principles of activity, in corporeal substances and in material powers, operate with motion on matter, and variously according to their various modes of operation.

If the so-called Positivists of modern times, who acknowledge no reality beyond that which is perceived by the senses, had known St. Thomas's sound and true principles of physics, they would not have identified the actions and passions of the sensitive and intelligent human soul with local motion. And those modern physicians, called Psychiatrians, who follow the foolish doctrines of the Positivists, would not have confused that which precedes madness, as a condition, with the disordered reason of a rational soul, and would not, by reducing all to mere motion, deserve to be thought mad themselves as well as mad-makers.

But the folly of modern science consists in admitting sensible facts only and condemning as an abuse the use of reason about those facts. This is destructive.

XVII.

THE PRINCIPLE, "QUOD MOVETUR AB ALIO MOVETUR, ET PRIMUM MOVENS EST IMMOBILE."

THIS principle of St. Thomas's school is of high importance and pregnant with the most momentous consequences. The scientists and philosophers of the modern sort do not even deign to notice it, but set it aside as an antiquated axiom of Peripatetic philosophy: and therefore they often fall into gross errors. Here we must remark that by the word *movetur* we mean, not only all bodies that are in local motion, but also every being whatsoever that by its motion, whatever it may be, passes from a potential to an actual state: for, as we have said, every change is motion.

In fact, when anything passes from potential being to actual being, its actual being is contingent, and might not have been. It therefore is a thing begun, an effect. But anything begun must have in its principle a sufficient reason of its being, as every effect has in its cause. This act therefore cannot have in itself the reason of its being, because if it could, the act, which as yet is not, would be its own cause. But that is impossible: therefore the cause of the act must be sought outside the act. That which moves the acting thing from being potential to being actual is *hoc ipso* not *in potentia* but *in actu*. But, if this mover were first potentially so, and then actually, it would *hoc ipso* require a sufficient reason of its own act, prior to that act in time, or at least in nature. This therefore can be repeated each time; and unless we stop at one that moves without passing from the potential to the actual, we shall have to admit an infinite series of movers and moved, because all these movers were potential before they were actual. But this infinite series is nonsense; firstly, because it would constitute in the concrete an infinite number, which is intrinsically absurd, and secondly because the whole series would be a thing reasoned on without a sufficient reason, and an effect without a cause. Therefore we must admit the existence of a First Mover Who is immoveable, i.e. immutable.

This is the Aristotelian argument by which we may rise to a knowledge of God, the Infinite, Necessary and therefore Immoveable or Immutable Being, Whose most beautiful definition, *Actus Purus*, given by Aristotle, was indicated by God Himself to Moses in the words, *Ego sum qui sum*, thereby excluding all potentiality; because that which is *in potentia* to be, cannot be said to BE, *simpliciter*, but will be what it will be by passing from potentially being to being actually.

If we consider existing things, we find that all are mutable because they are contingent, and therefore that all of them, in order to pass from potentially being to actually being, need to be moved by God, the Immoveable First Mover.

But created things, it may be said, are animate and inanimate. Inanimate things, that cannot move themselves, evidently, as you say, depend on something else to be moved or changed by: and unless we go on *ad infinitum* with a fantastic series of movers and moved, we must come at last to a supreme immoveable Mover, who is God. But living creatures move themselves, and therefore do not require to be moved by another, having in themselves the principle of their motion.

But we say in reply that a living creature does not move itself *secundum se totum*. One part moves the other, or one faculty is moved by another. Hence in the living creature there is the moved and there is the mover. But how about that which in the living creature is the mover? Is that immoveable?

Or is it first a mover *in potentia* and then an actual mover? Evidently the latter; and therefore the motion of living creatures is primarily caused by the Immoveable First Mover, God.

God moves everything according to its nature. Irrational things He moves by determining them to particular objects; either because they are quite without knowledge, or because they have only a sensitive knowledge of particulars. In these therefore God determines the *potentia* to the act. Moreover He moves, and by causing determines, the will of rational creatures to the good which is their specific object, and which the intellect knows in the Universal. The will therefore cannot in its acts tend otherwise than to that which has in itself some reason of being good in a universal sense. Now since Almighty God, by causing, determines the will to the universal *ratio* of Good, the will would in fact be quite determined by God, if the object that adequately and fully contains the universal *ratio* of the Good were manifested to the intellect; but when the object manifested to the intellect presents a limited participation of Good, the will is not then determined by Him. It then is free. It may either not choose the particular good, or (inasmuch as it is not determined by God to that limitation of Good which it knows in the particular) it may determine itself to choose that limitation of good. Therefore, when the will chooses a finite *bonum*, it must always be said to have been moved by God, because moved it was by Him to the Universal *Bonum* without determination to the particular. We must observe, however, that since the will can never, in its acts, go beyond its own specific object, which is the Good to which it is determined by God, it never can reject a particular good as a good, but only as limited and therefore deprived of greater good; thus by reason of this privation, being an evil, and therefore not within the sphere of its formal and specific object, which is the Good. In rejecting evil, the will inclines to its contrary—good, whereto it is moved by God, Who, as its Mover, inclines it always to the Good, which more or less is to be found in every particular object whatsoever. When a man sins, he wills the sin by reason of its being an apparent good, which he apprehends therein; and God moves him to this *ratio* of good, while the disordered will freely wills the bad object that participates of it. Thus it is that God, as the first Immoveable Mover, moves and determines the will to its specific object—the universal Good, apprehended in every particular object,—but does not determine it to sin.

From this we can see that, although the inclination or motion towards the Universal Good never can be repudiated by the will, because without that it cannot will anything, nevertheless this inclination and motion is not in fact necessitated or determined at the presence of any finite good, (as it is at the presence of the Infinite Good, in which the whole *ratio* of good is contained,) but is in proportion to that limited *ratio* of good which the particular object presents. Therefore the Angelic Doctor writes as follows: He says firstly: *Deus movet voluntatem hominis, sicut universalis motor, ad universale objectum voluntatis, quod est bonum; et sine hoc universali motione homo non potest aliquid velle, sed homo per rationem determinat se ad volendum hoc, vel illud, quod est vere bonum, vel apparens bonum.* * This motion cannot be called universal except so far as it regards all the motions that God gives to all the singular acts. The universal *bonum* is the *ratio boni* to which the will must tend in every particular act. By *sine hoc*, &c., he points out, not that it must precede in time every act whatsoever of the will, but that it necessarily is to be found in every act of the will. *Determinat se*, &c., &c., means, that with this *in sensu composto*, Divine motion moving it, the will

---

* 1ᵃ 2ᵃᵉ Q. ix. a. 6 ad 3.

determines *itself* to each particular *bonum*, and therefore that the Divine Motion is not the determinator.

In the *Quæstiones Disputatæ* * St. Thomas expresses the same conception thus: *Natura rationalis, quæ est Deo vicinissima, non solum habet inclinationem in aliquid sicut habent inanimata, nec solum movens hanc inclinationem quasi aliunde eis determinatam, sicut natura sensibilis; sed ultra hoc habet in potestate ipsam inclinationem, ut non sit ei necessarium inclinari ad appetibile apprehensum,* SED POSSIT INCLINARI VEL NON INCLINARI; *et sic ipsa inclinatio* NON DETERMINATUR *ei* AB ALIO, SED A SEIPSA. This means that when the intellect apprehends a particular and sees in it a *ratio boni*, (to which God moves us, the *ratio boni* being the formal and specific object of the will,) then the will is inclined thereby to the participated good in the particular object; but such inclining does not *determine* the will to the said particular object. The intellect may think of something else that has some *ratio boni*, and experiencing in the will the Divine inclining, choose the same: or it may think of other things.

Hence, on this most important point, St. Thomas tells us that, when the will is *in potentia* to act, i.e., is not acting, it cannot

---

* Q. xxii. *De Veritate*, De appetitu boni et voluntate, a. 4.

be moved by itself alone. God, the First immoveable Mover, moves it, not as He moves irrational beings, but, as its rational nature requires, determining it to its universal or formal object, the Good, i.e. the *ratio boni*; but not determining it to those finite participations of Good, or of the *ratio boni*, which are found in particulars.

After this exposition of the great principle that *quod movetur*, i.e., what passes from the potential to the actual, *ab alio movetur*, and that the *primum movens*, i.e. God, *est immobile*, we can appreciate that wonderful saying of the Angelic Doctor, that all created nature is the instrument of God. *Instrumentum enim est causa quodammodo effectus principalis causæ, non per formam vel virtutem propriam, sed in quantum participat aliquid de virtute principalis causæ per motum ejus, sicut dolabra non est causa rei artificiatæ per formam vel virtutem propriam, sed per virtutem artificis a quo movetur et eam quoquomodo participat.** But though the principal cause moves the instrumental, the latter does something in accordance with its own nature. *Nisi res naturales aliquid agerent, frustra essent eis formæ et virtutes naturales collatæ; sicut si cultellus non incideret, frustra haberet acumen.* †

While showing that all creatures are

---

* *Quæst. Disp.* iii., *De Pot.*, a. 9.   † Ibid.

instruments of God, though they operate according to their own virtues, we must carefully consider how God operates in all things and applies them to their operations. St. Thomas, with an angelic penetration, teaches us that God is the cause of all Being, and that creatures determine the mode of the Divine Causality. *Secundum ordinem causarum,* he says, *est ordo effectuum. Primum autem in omnibus effectibus est esse; nam omnia alia sunt determinationes ipsius. Igitur esse est proprius effectus primi agentis, et omnia alia agunt ipsum in quantum agunt in virtute primi agentis; secunda autem agentia, quæ sunt quasi particulantia et determinantia actionem primi agentis, agunt sicut proprios effectus alias perfectiones quæ determinant esse.** The attributes of Being are the True and the Good: and because *omne ens est verum, et omne esse est bonum,* these are the two transcendental attributes of Being. Hence when any intellect tends to the true, that tendency is the effect of the first Mover, God, and is particularized and determined by the intellect embracing this or that truth: and when any appetite—intellective, sensitive, or natural—tends to the Good, this tendency will be an effect of the first Agent, God, which is particularized and determined to this or that *bonum*. The first

---

* *Contra Gent.*, iii. 66.

Mover will always be the immediate cause of the tendency to Being, which is true and good. Therefore, while the secondary agent particularizes and determines that tendency, God applies it to the True and the Good.

But this particularizing or determining will be necessary in some cases, free in others. When the particularizing must be one, it will be necessary. When it may be manifold, it will not be necessary. If the form with which the object is apprehended is of one particular object only, there cannot be a choice of more: and therefore there is a necessary actuation to that particular object whereto the First Mover moves it: but if the form by which the object is presented is the *Bonum Universale*, clearly the agent cannot be necessitated to a particular *bonum*, because that form may answer to an indefinite number of things. Now, whenever a man uses his reason, a corporeal singular *bonum* is presented in sense or in imagination. But then, together with that, the reason of the Universal *Bonum* is apprehended by the intellect, because the singular is known indirectly by a sort of reflection, and in it is known a limited participation of Good universally, of which the intellect has the idea. Therefore, since the will follows the intellect, which would be determined *per se* and necessitated, if the total *ratio boni* were presented in the concrete *bonum*, the will must remain not determined, but free,—free to determine itself to any object whatsoever that may present itself as having some participation of Good.

Therefore, as the fact that God is the Infinite Being and the First Being does not exclude created beings, who participate of Being, from existing in their singularity, neither does the fact of His being the first and universal Cause prevent the existence of secondary causes diversely participating of the first and universal Causality. Hence in a recent work, *Concordia tra la libertà e la divina mozione*, the author, following St. Thomas, laid down the Divine Moving towards the Universal *Bonum* as the specific and universal object of the human will; and he proved that the will freely particularizes and determines the Divine motion itself to particular objects or *bona*, so that the tendency impressed by God to the Universal *ratio boni* is the same tendency with which the will freely determines itself to the participated *ratio*, limited to the particular object. St. Thomas, as the above-quoted author shows, admits that God may also move us in a particular manner to a particular *bonum:* but this is an exception. God does not, in that case, act as *Motor Universalis.** This much, I think, is

---

* Giovanni Maria Cornoldi, S.J., *Quale secondo San Tommaso, sia la concordia della Mozione Divina colla libertà umana.*

sufficient in explanation of the principle that whatever is moved is moved by something else, and that the first Mover is immoveable.

Roma, 1890. Against this demonstration we have not as yet heard any important objection.

XVIII.

THE MUTABILITY OF EXTENSION.

DESCARTES asserted that the extension of corporeal substances is *per se* immutable; nor could he say otherwise after denying substantial forms, in which there is the principle or sufficient reason of the changes of that extension. Now, if we admit the mutability of extension, many facts in nature can be explained, which if it be denied, can only be cut like the Gordian knot. This has, in fact, been experienced by his followers. They could not explain nature consistently with the principle of reasoning; and therefore they must either content themselves with a merely historic or empirical description of nature, or else ignore the principles of reasoning, sometimes admitting action truly at a distance, and sometimes putting forward effects of which, in that system, no proportionate cause could be assigned; which comes to the same thing as denying it. Thus we find that, in the explanation of certain phenomena belonging to proper expansion, some modern scientists, who insist on explaining them by improper expansion only and deny the variability of real volumes, fall back pitiably on ridiculous hypotheses.

Let us here examine the arguments used against us. The first and strongest is a question of reasoning. "Compenetration of corporeal substances," they say, "is repugnant to reason: but without that there cannot be such a thing as proper mutability of extension in a corporeal substance. Therefore, such mutability is repugnant to reason."

In reply we must begin by referring back to what we said* about the real and apparent volume of corporeal substances, and why, when treating of the mutability of extension, we must have regard to the former, not to the latter. Even our adversaries admit that a porous body can expand or contract by increase or diminution of its pores, in number or in size: but they deny that a corporeal substance, individual and therefore continuous, can, without having pores, dilate, and while retaining the continuity, become more extended. Thus the question before us is about continuous substances, and not about aggregates of substances.

Having premised thus much, let us come to the major of their argument, viz., that compenetration of corporeal substances is repugnant

---
* Chapter VI.

to reason. What, we ask, do you mean by compenetration? "It means," they say, "that one corporeal substance is occupying the same place actually occupied by another." Granted, but we deny its being repugnant to reason. The contradictory alone—viz., its being and not being at the same time—is repugnant to reason, because negation only is irreconcilable with affirmation. If therefore compenetration of corporeal substances is repugnant to reason, we should have to say that, in consequence of the compenetration, the substance loses its own essence and ceases to be. Now this cannot be shown, for the essence of a body does not require for itself only a determinate place. The body requires that by reason of its local quantity: and local quantity is an accident not essential to the body but merely natural, and therefore may, by the omnipotence of God, be taken away in a particular case. This is demonstrated by those philosophers who, keeping to the true principles of reasoning, instead of being led by fancy, do not suppose that nothing is true except what is perceived by the senses.

Two bodies therefore can be in the same place, provided that both, or at least one of them, be deprived of local quantity, which has an extrinsic regard to excluding from its own place any other substance that has local quantity. Hence a philosopher may say that compenetration of corporeal substances is not natural, but he cannot say that it is absurd.

It is no answer to say, "I can't conceive such a thing," for a personal want of power to understand can never be a criterion of what is intrinsically repugnant or not repugnant to reason. If so, we should have to reject many indubitable truths as repugnant to reason. The human mind cannot create. It only copies. This means that it cannot well conceive things of which nature does not furnish the species. Therefore of all those things that are beyond or outside the order fixed in nature, and are called supernatural or preternatural, it has but weak and ill-proportioned conceptions, formed almost always by mere analogy. However much we may show by force of argument, that true compenetration is not repugnant to reason, it nevertheless is beyond the order fixed in nature: and therefore it is difficult for the mind of man to form a clear conception of it.

Let us now come to the minor, in which the weak part of the objection is.

"There cannot be such a thing," they say, "as mutability of extension without compenetration." This is false. Compenetration means the simultaneous occupation of one place by more than one body, each of which occupies the whole of it. The mutability implies contraction, which merely requires that one point in the mutable thing should happen to occupy the space left free by another that occupied it before. Thus compenetration differs from contraction as the simultaneous from the successive : and therefore if contraction takes place where there is mutability, compenetration does not. Let us make the conclusion clearer to sense by considering two points, *a* and *b*, of one continuous individual substance, as near to each other as you like.

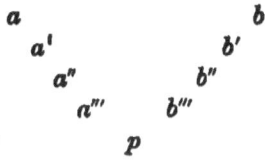

Given the gradual contraction of the substance, *a* and *b* will tend continually to approach each other : but will they ever compenetrate? Certainly not, unless we say that the extension of the substance is not merely diminished by condensing, but quite lost by reducing itself to a mathematical point. Therefore *a* and *b* will never compenetrate in *p*: but the distance between them will diminish as

$$a'\ b',\ a''\ b'',\ a'''\ b''',$$

according to the measure of its contraction, the distance becoming continually less. This is founded on the principle that, inasmuch as we can conceive a quantity always increasing, though never becoming infinite, so can we conceive a quantity always diminishing but never quite destroyed by mere diminution. What we have said about the substance between these points, a and b, applies equally to any other particle of a continuous substance, and shows that contraction can take place without compenetration.

It is easy therefore to perceive why our opponents persist in saying that mutability of extension implies compenetration. They cannot conceive contraction first, and then local transposition, but only think of the transposition. Thus, for instance, they imagine a continuous spherical substance, which condenses in such a manner that each of its least particles, while remaining as it was, approaches the centre where, with the others, it agglomerates. According to this hypothesis there would be no real contraction of the spherical substance, but only a transposition of each part; which assuredly could not take place without a true compenetration. We say advisedly, "*real* contraction;" for though the substance would then seem to be more restricted than before, its entity would not be really condensed, but only transposed, as the real surface of a piece of paper is (to make use of a similitude) not diminished by being folded up into a smaller visible size. A particle therefore of the spherical substance cannot, while preserving its former extension, be transferred into the centre without occupying the place of what was there before—in other words, not without compenetration. But such is not true condensation as taught in the Physical system. According to that each particle of the substance contracts within itself entitatively; so that its whole entity is contracted in one way; and the act of contraction does not require that any particle placed on the surface should break off and transfer itself elsewhere. Nay, as a part of one and the same substance, it will always be conjoined thereto, continuing to form with the whole a continuous substance in its decreasing extension: and thus only it does not keep the space first occupied, but approaches the centre. Therefore, if we conceive in this manner, firstly contraction in the entity itself and then translocation of all the particles that compose it, there is no danger of having to admit true compenetration. If likeness will clear the conception, we can find it in any object that, when seen through a more or less powerful microscope, shows its mass, either more extended without disjunction of parts, or more restricted without compenetration of the parts. Thus the minor proposition of our adversary's argument will not stand, and therefore its conclusion falls to the ground.

And now we come to another difficulty objected against us—a question of fact, put in this way: "All bodies are porous; and therefore the mutability of extension cannot be admitted. The *antecedens* is proved from innumerable experiences. The *consequens* cannot be denied, because in that case all condensation of substance would be effected by diminution of pores, all rarefaction from their becoming enlarged: so that we must reject all mutability of extension as useless."

This argument is clear. Let us examine it. The *antecedens* may be conceded: for though it is not the result of an adequate deduction, the proofs in favour of all bodies being porous are such and so many, that it may be prudently affirmed as a universal proposition. Not however as it seems to be understood by the followers of the Mechanic system, in which each atom is so isolated that it comes not in contact with its neighbouring atoms at any part. Setting aside other reasons, one fails to see how, according to that opinion, we could possibly affirm and explain the entitative unity of individual substances, especially the animated, which are not mere aggregates.

As to the *consequens*—viz., "All bodies are porous, and therefore true mutability of extension must be excluded"—it will not pass muster in good logic. Granted that by mere mutation of pores the bodies furnished with them can be rarefied or condensed, it does not legitimately follow that all condensation and rarefaction must depend on mutation of pores. In the exposition of the Physical system we admitted that, besides the *proper* condensation and rarefaction produced by true change of extension, there is the *improper*, which is produced by a change in the interstices called pores. This distinction was well known among the Scholastics: and thereby, as Toledo remarks, the followers of Aristotle were distinguished from those of Democritus and Epicurus. *Antiqui non cognoscebant nisi hanc solam (sc. impropriam), cum hoc discrimine, quod illi ponebant intra corpora poros, nos vero plenos subtiliore corpore. Alia est condensatio et rarefactio propria, et hæc non fit corporis alterius expulsione vel receptione, sed mutatione ipsius subjecti.*[*]

"But there is an axiom," it will be said, "that we must not multiply beings *(entia)* without necessity: therefore since pores will sufficiently explain the whole thing, away with the mutability of extension." Our answer is this:

Firstly, the argument may be turned against the objector. Given the mutability of extension, the whole thing can be explained, and

---

[*] *In IV. Ph.*, c. 9, Q. xi.

much better. Therefore, what is the use of supposing such and so many discontinuing pores everywhere? Secondly, our opponent proceeds *a posse ad esse*, and therefore *non valet illatio*. It comes to this: "We can explain everything by the theory of pores. Therefore that theory is the only true one, and all others are false."

Nego. There are many phenomena that may be explained in various ways. What right therefore has anyone to insist on one only in this case, excluding mutability of extension, though it serves its purpose well? Thirdly, the axiom quoted against the mutability of extension is not applicable, unless the objector had first proved that Almighty God could not have a suitable end for so endowing corporeal substances. This he would find very hard to do. Fourthly, the pores do not explain everything. This I conclusively proved in another work.*

We may therefore legitimately conclude, I think, that the objections cited are not valid. I have not met with others of any weight.

* *Filosofia Scolastica;* Fisica Razionale particolare, Parte i. Lezioni xli. xlii.

XIX.

WHY THE PHYSICAL SYSTEM IS SUPPOSED TO BE IN OPPOSITION TO PHYSICS.

SOME people will have it that the Physical system is opposed to physics, because the principles of geometry had been believed to show that no body is continuous, each being composed of mathematical points and therefore quite indivisible. This opinion was refuted by Aristotle. The supporters of it said, "What is a solid? The sum of the superficies. And what is the superficies? The sum of lines. And what is the line? The sum of many points. Therefore a solid is constituted by points, and is not continuous."

But the falseness of this reasoning is evident. In geometry a line is not considered as an aggregate of points, which, unless they touched one another, would not form it, and if they did touch, would coincide in one point only; for *indivisibilia aut non se tangunt, aut se tangunt juxta se tota.* A line is conceived *ut excursio puncti,* as an imaginary track leaving nothing of itself except the point that slips away. Thus we may suppose geometrically that a superficies is derived from excursion of lines, and a solid from excursion of superficies. But though we may consider a mathematical point as a limit of a line, we may not say that it can exist by itself. These are fictions of the imagination: but solid bodies are real, and therefore cannot be constituted by indivisible points.

Hence it is evident that, since the Dynamic system, which supposes the extended and the solid to be constituted by unextended forces in mathematical points, is repugnant to reason: the Physical system, which admits the extended and the real continuous, accords with the sure testimony of the senses, by which we perceive things that are extended, and that, as such, must have a certain continuity.

In attacking the Physical system, the adversaries of St. Thomas and of the Scholastics put forth a specious but sophistical argument. "If," they say, "we grant that a body is extended and continuous, we cannot avoid admitting that a particle of it is infinite; which cannot be maintained without an evident contradiction. The real extended, if there is such a thing, must be divisible into the extended whose extension ever decreases. Therefore a small part has an infinite number of parts: and so that small part will be infinite, because an extended thing that includes an infinite number of extended things cannot be said to be finite."

To make this question clear we must clearly understand the divisibility of the continuous extended.

XX.

ON THE DIVISIBILITY OF THE CONTINUOUS EXTENDED.

FIRST of all we must know the difference between an entitative or real distinction and a mere distinction of reason. When two entities can really be divided from each other, or so separated that one or both continue to exist, we certainly must affirm that there is a real distinction between them, and not a mere distinction of reason. There cannot be any question about that; for if it were only a distinction of reason, there would be a real identity, the one would really be the other. Both would be the *idem*. But the *idem* cannot really be divided into parts that continue to exist independently of each other; just as a mathematical point cannot be divided into two points. That division therefore is a sure sign of real distinction.

But though this real divisibility shows a previously real distinction between the divisibles, it is not the only sign. We can deduce the real distinction otherwise. Now because what is here indicated is a true criterion, we say firstly, that the parts of an extended substance are really distinct, because by a finite or infinite virtue they are really divisible; secondly, that the *potentia* is really distinct from its *actus*, because it may be separated therefrom. The matter, for instance, may be separated from the form, the intellect from the determinate act of understanding, the will from the volition, the soul from virtue and grace, a substance from its accidents. But we must bear in mind that, although the divisibility of two things essentially supposes a real distinction between them, nevertheless the conception of the real distinction is essentially different from the conception of the divisibility, and *a fortiori* different from the conception of the division. To confound them together and identify them would be absurd.

Certainly then, in the continuous, the parts are really but indeterminately distinct, and so long as the parts are not divided, either really or in the mind, it is not a discrete quantity. Whence it follows that the parts of the continuous have in reality no number; therefore it is absurd to speak of the continuous as having an infinite number of parts, though we can conceive it as infinitely divisible, and mentally imagine it as divided into numerable and numbered parts.

To make our meaning clear, we must distinguish the mathematical continuity from physical continuity. In mathematics the continuous is the continuous quantity mentally abstracted from the real substance or body which is the subject of the same. In physics the continuous is this or that substance or body with the quantity whose subject it is. Have both or has either infinite parts?

To this we reply that in the mathematical continuous, just because it is not a discrete quantity, there are no parts, finite or infinite, *in actu*, but there are infinite parts *in potentia*. In the physical continuous there are no parts, finite or infinite, *in actu*, but there are finite, not infinite, parts *in potentia*.

That in the mathematical continuous there are no parts *in actu*, either finite or infinite, but only finite parts *in potentia*, is evident. A small quantity, being essentially extended, can never be reduced to such a state by division that at one part it should be an extended thing, and at the other a mathematical point, or that an extended thing should be divisible into two mathematical points. The continuous quantity therefore will be essentially divisible into extended parts ever divisible: so that we never can consider as impossible a further division. Thus the mathematical continuous is *in potentia* essentially divisible *ad infinitum*. The infinite is the goal or term that we never can reach. In that term each part would be unextended : $\frac{1}{\infty} = 0$.

The physical continuous is not mere quantity. It is the solid substance in which, as in a subject, the quantity is; and therefore the quantity cannot be divided without dividing the substance. If we consider the mere quantity, we find the continuous divisible *ad infinitum* potentially and not actually; but having to consider the substance also, we must say that the physical continuous is neither actually nor potentially divisible *ad infinitum*. Some people tell us that a division *ad infinitum* is impossible because a substance, unless it were infinite, could not be capable of such a division. Others think that this is a paradox; for they cannot understand how in the continuous the division can stop, seeing that the continuous is *quantum*, and that quantity is *per se* divisible *ad infinitum*. But we have to see whether this impossibility of dividing the physical continuous *ad infinitum*, which cannot be derived from the *ratio* of quantity, can be derived from the *ratio* of substance, or of the concrete nature of divisible being. The Angelic Doctor tells us that it is so derived.

For every corporeal nature must be considered, firstly, in its intrinsic essence, and secondly in what we may call its extrinsication, by which it stretches out to occupy a place and impede occupation of the same place by any other body. This latter property originates from the substance itself as a force or virtue of it. We can easily conceive a minimum of extension, at which a corporeal substance is no longer able to extend itself, occupy a place and resist the occupation of the same place by other substances. "It must be understood," says St. Thomas, "that a body, which is complete in size, is to be considered in two ways, i.e. mathematically, or according to the quantity alone, and naturally, by considering in it the matter and the form. It is evident that a natural body cannot be infinite *in actu*. For every natural body has some determinate substantial form: and therefore, since accidents follow the substantial form, determinate accidents, one of which is quantity, must follow a determinate substantial form. Therefore every natural body has a determinate quantity for the greater and for the less."* Hence he quotes elsewhere *(Comm. in II. Sent.*, Distinct. xxx. Q. ii. a. 2) those words of Aristotle: *Ideo est invenire minimam aquam et minimam carnem, quæ si dividatur,*

---

* *Summa*, P. i. Q. vii. a. 3.

non erit ulterius aqua et caro. Therefore, whether the body be elementary, e.g., gold, oxygen and the rest, or a compound of elementary substances, e.g. water, wood, marble, &c., we shall come, in thought at least, to a limit at which it could not be divided again without ceasing to have force or virtue sufficient for co-extending and for resisting the occupation of its place by any other body. In other words, it would cease to have quantity, and *remota quantitate, substantia omnis indivisibilis est.* [*]

According to this doctrine we have, both in elementary and composite bodies, true atoms, i.e. the smallest that can be; and we may fairly suppose that not mere mixtures, but true chemical combinations, in which the nature of the substance is changed, are made with the smallest corporeal substances. Now these *minima*, which, if again divided, would cease to have quantity and no longer be divisible, must have volume and weight, and be in a certain number, and occupy certain relative positions. Surely then it cannot be said that we Thomists are far from agreeing to those laws of chemistry which lay down that chemical combinations require the elementary substances to be in a certain number, in a certain volume, in a certain weight, and that, in

---

[*] *Contra Gent.*, iv. 65.

combining, they must have a previously determined relative position according to the nature of each. But these laws must not be arbitrarily presupposed. They must be founded on facts or on well proved reasoning, or not be presupposed.

XXI.

ETHER.

WHAT we have said about corporeal substance divisible into particles that are most minute, substantially indivisible, and therefore real atoms, reminds us of what is said and what was said about ether. The most common opinion among the scientists of our time is, firstly, that in the interplanetary spaces there is a corporeal substance extremely rarified: secondly, that this rarefaction consists in the mutual distance of the atoms from each other, which distance, compared with the length of the diameters of these atoms, is so great that (proportions considered) it is as the distance of the stars and the planets from each other: lastly, that the nature of these ethereal atoms is the same in all, and is not different from that of the corporeal atoms in this world; so that the ethereal atoms may be said to be the terrestrial atoms themselves extremely diminished and very far from each other. They say too that this ethereal substance is the subject whence light, electricity and heat are diffused. One of the defects observable in modern scientists is their ignorance of many doctrines, often true and important, which the old scientists knew. Hence it is not surprising to hear them say that the conception of ether is modern. In the *Cosmos*, a French periodical, * Courbet says: " La conception d'une substance transmettant la lumière et remplissant l'espace a été introduite pour la première fois dans la science moderne par Hugghens." This *pour la première fois* is historically a blunder. We had better point out the discrepancy between the ancient and modérn scientists about the ether.

1°. The modern scientists acknowledge the existence of ether in the interplanetary spaces for the purpose of giving a subject to light and heat; but for the very same reason the old scientists acknowledged the necessity of an ethereal substance. " Aristotle," says St. Thomas, "rejected that error (which denied the existence of ether, and admitted a void), but said that Democritus was wrong in affirming that, if the space between the eye and the object were quite void, we should be able to see the smallest object at an immeasurable distance,—for instance, an ant in the sky. This is totally impossible.

---

* An. 1890, xvi. p. 154, &c.

"We cannot see, unless the organ of sight receives an impression from a visible object: but it has been shown that this impression is not received immediately from the visible external objects; and therefore that there must be a medium substance between the sight and the visible thing. If there were a void, there would be no medium capable of being immuted and immuting: so that, if there were an absolute void, we should not see. Democritus fell into the mistake, because he believed that distance impedes our sight of an object just so much as that which is between impedes the operation of the visible thing: but this is false. The reason why distance impedes the sight is this: All bodies are seen under a certain angle of some triangle, or rather of a pyramid, whose base is in the seen object, and the angle is in the eye of the seer. (*Omne corpus videtur sub quodam angulo cujusdam trianguli, vel magis pyramidis, cujus basis est in re visa, et angulus est in oculo videntis.*) Therefore the greater the object is, compared with the size of the pupil, the more diminished proportionately must the immutation of that visible object be when it comes to the sight. It is evident then that the longer the sides of the triangle or of the pyramid are, the size of the base remaining fixed, the less will the angle be. Therefore the further the object is, the less do we see; and the distance may be so great that we cannot see it at all."*

From this it is evident that the old scientists admitted interplanetary ethereal substance; that they did not admit the system of emission of light; that they judged light to be not a substance; that they believed it to be a quality derived from a luminous body in the ether, a quality that makes an impression on the pupil, which is enabled thereby to see the object from which that quality is derived by means of the ether, and that the ethereal medium is necessary for seeing, whether the object be far or near. The Angelic Doctor said that *omnis lux est effectiva caloris, etiam lux lunæ*,† some centuries before Melloni said so. Evidently therefore it was admitted then that the ethereal substance transmitted heat and was the subject of the medium of heat.

2°. The modern scientists commonly admit, as we pointed out before, that the ethereal substance is an aggregation of atoms very distant from each other, if the distance be compared with their diameter: but they maintain the system of undulations, according to which these atoms oscillate in lines parallel to

---

* *De anima*, II. Lect. 15.
† *In II. Sent.*, Dist. xv. Q. 1. a. 2 ad 5.

each other and vertical to the luminous ray. There is a difficulty in this that seems to us insuperable: for if the atoms oscillated, they could never come in contact with each other and determine in the others the motion supposed to be given by the luminous object. Hence we should not be able to explain the illumination without the absurdity of admitting collision at a true distance. The Scholastics, as we said, acknowledged a true and proper dilation of the corporeal substances, and not merely the improper: so they never fell into the absurdity of admitting action of ethereal atoms at a true distance. They were indeed very far from having certain experiences that modern scientists have: but the latter are very far from having a perfect knowledge of the nature of things, from which facts ought to be derived.

3°. Many modern scientists hold that the ethereal substance is the very substance of the earth and of the air extremely rarefied by the distance between the atoms: and therefore action at a distance is not the only difficulty to be objected against them. There are others, for such an ethereal substance ought to have the principal properties of the other corporeal substances—that of resisting other bodies—retarding motion, coming into combination with them, &c. Hence the modern author whom we quoted from *The Cosmos*, is much embarrassed, and believing himself to have shown that the ethereal substance cannot be at all suspected of the least resistance to the planetary bodies, concludes thus : " Nous sommes en présence de deux affirmations absolument opposées. Il n'y a pas de milieu matériel dans l'espace (Hirn, Faye). Il est sûr que l'espace est rempli d'un milieu capable d'être en vibration, l'éther (Hertz)." Hence Courbet, strangely and without sufficient reason, would introduce into science an opinion taken from Theology, where it teaches that the glorified bodies have the gift of being subtle or penetrable, not resisting earthly bodies nor resisted by them. He says that, if it be necessary, science may without discredit get light from faith, to solve insuperable difficulties in questions of nature.

In the olden time they did not ask whether the ethereal substance resisted the stars and retarded their course, because the conceptions about that were not those of the vulgar. They did not believe it to have the nature of earthly bodies, solid or aerial : did not believe in the possibility of its combining with such and changing its nature. Therefore it was said to be unalterable. The ethereal substance was the firmament. It was not the stars, but that *in* which the stars are placed, according to the first chapter of Genesis: *Fecitque Deus duo luminaria magna. . . . et stellas, et posuit eas in firmamento cœli.*

St. Thomas, in answer to the question, *Utrum firmamentum sit de natura inferiorum corporum*, replies that before Aristotle all the philosophers believed the firmament or heaven to be a substance like in nature to the elementary bodies of this world. Aristotle, he says, proved that the firmament or heaven has not a nature common to other bodies, but has a proper essence: and the later philosophers, persuaded by his reasoning, admitted his doctrine. According to this doctrine the substance of the firmament, in which the stars are, is not heavy, does not alter nor corrupt: and since it has not even a common matter with the other bodies, we cannot, he says *(De natura generis)*, form a conception of it univocally with other bodies, but only an analagous conception. In these days, as in those, we are a long way from having a sure knowledge of the essence of the ethereal substance or firmament; and though we can affirm in accordance with the doctrine above mentioned, that it is the medium and the subject whence light and heat come (as is hinted in the Book of Genesis), we still hesitate, incapable of solving the grave difficulties put forward by Courbet in *The Cosmos*.

XXII.

CHEMISTRY.

THIS is a most important and arduous question, owing to its intrinsic difficulty and the discrepancy of opinion about it. So long as chemistry remains within the limits of its own natural boundaries, collecting facts and registering phenomena, the learned cannot really be at variance with each other, though there may be more or less exactness in explaining and more or less faithful accounts of things: but when, passing these limits, it takes to deciding philosophically about the nature and essence of things, then it is that discrepancies arise. This happens, in some cases, through deficient knowledge of philosophy and a want of sound logic, while in others it proceeds from the modern fashion of following experience only, and confusing the senses with reason. We must therefore be very cautious, ready to receive all facts that are clearly proved, to admit the principles that are absolutely connected with those facts, and then enquire whether such are the principles accepted in the philosophy of St. Thomas.

Chemistry is the science that treats of the substantial changes in bodies. A substantial change means that which happens when a substance is changed, not by mere variation of temperature, nor by the fleeting influence of extrinsic agents, but by a change in its inmost being, so that it changes its nature, and, instead of being what it was, becomes another substance. Such mutation takes place in corporeal substances only, because they alone have a composite essence: and since our minds have no immediate intuition of substances, but know them through their operations, the diversity or contrariety of these operations will guide us to discern whether or no their substantial being is changed. This does not require a change in all the operations. It is enough to know that the specific operations have changed: for since the genus remains in the substantial mutations of corporeal things, the operations or passions belonging to the genus itself must remain. Hence a substance may change into another and yet have the same gravity, the same weight, the same solidity or liquidness, &c. It is very difficult sometimes to be sure of a substantial change, but we often can be sure of it. Knowing, for instance, that substances without life are different from living substances, we cannot doubt that inorganic minerals, when changed into plants or into sentient things, are substantially changed. This may, sometimes at least, be extended beyond the living, without fear of falling into error.

The proper and principal object, therefore, of chemistry is to be found in those substantial changes, obtained by combination of elements, which all modern scientists call chemical combination. The accidental changes of substances, called alterations, are but a secondary object accidentally treated of in chemistry. Herein there seems to be no essential discrepancy between the doctrine of St. Thomas and the true principles of modern science, together with the facts that chemists have shown to be certain. But the modern doctrine is in disagreement with that of many old physicists, and also of some modern ones, who put forward, without any sound reason, principles founded on their own fancy, or facts that do not exist. We must therefore discuss elementary substances according to our own doctrines distinctly.

XXIII.

ELEMENTARY ATOMS.

AN elementary substance is an atom which, essentially composed of *materia prima* and substantial form, is simple, inasmuch as it does not result from a chemical combination of different substances. The word "atom" does not in itself indicate a smallest and indivisible substance, but a substance not constituted by aggregation of substances. This meaning is evidently right. An aggregate, though specifically one, cannot be called individually one, because it results from the union of many substances, whether their nature be the same, or not. By thus using the word "atom," we are in no danger of falling into what is called the atomic theory; for in that system, strictly speaking, the atoms are inert, of equal nature, essentially extended, only capable of moving and being moved, and quantitatively indivisible. But they are not so in the Physical system.

Applying then to elementary substances the

known principles that we have pointed out, we must say that it is essentially composed of *materia prima* and substantial form. Being essentially extended, it must have the principle of extension; and the principle of extension is what we call *materia prima*. The substantial form is the principle of that virtue or activity which determines the specific nature of the substance, which principle cannot be essentially wanting in that elementary substance. Suppose, for instance, that oxygen, sulphur, hydrogen and carbon are, as we now believe them to be, elementary substances, specifically different. We learn their specific diversity from the divers and constant virtues, observable in their mutual operations, that chemistry shows plainly by facts within our reach: and we should look for them in vain elsewhere. Since therefore a specific activity is evident in these atoms, there must be a principle of that activity. But this is precisely what places them in different species, making the nature of hydrogen to be the nature of hydrogen, and not the nature of gold or of something else. There being then, in such atoms a principle of activity, we must admit a substantial form; that is, the said principle.

In discussing the principle of activity we have placed the elements in mutual relation: but that was for the purpose of making the argument more easily intelligible. If oxygen were the only thing in the corporeal world, it would have its *materia prima* and substantial form just as it has now when existing among other elementary substances; for with its extension it would have the principle of extension, and with its activity, (existing *in potentia*, at least,) it would have the principle of activity, i.e. the substantial form. We say *in potentia*, because, being inorganic, it could not operate on itself, so that if no other body of a different nature existed in the world, there would be no subject in which the potential activity could be brought into action.

The matter and form of the elements cannot be mingled in one principle. They are essentially two principles, *really* distinct. In this question we have to steer between two extremes, one of them sinning by excess, the other by defect. We should go into excess by imagining that *materia prima* is a substance constituted *per se* in its own being, and that every substantial form is a simple being, subsistent *per se*, and only operating on *materia prima*. Were it so, the form would not be substantial and informant, because it would not constitute the matter in substantial being. It would only be a *forma assistens*, not being by its own essence united to the matter, but only by the operation.

In short, there the atom would have two complete substances in its own being, instead of being, as it is, *one* substance.

To consider the principles of extension and of activity as one being, in the absurd guise of a matter *per se* active or a force *per se* extended, would be sinning by defect.

Consequently we must affirm that in the elementary substances *materia prima*, though really distinct from the substantial form, is not separate from it. The true and philosophic meaning of these two expressions is well known. Two things are really separate when each has its complete being, and is the principle of its own operation. They are really distinct when each has a being *per se* incomplete, and each is not *per se* a principle of operation. Suppose, for instance, a waxen image of Cæsar. The image is not separate from the wax, for the very wax is the image: but distinct it is, because otherwise the wax could not be fashioned into any other image. But, between the pen that writes and the hand that holds it, there is something more than a real distinction; because the pen, though moved as an instrument by the hand, has a substantial and complete being, different from that of the hand. Here there is not a real distinction only. The pen is the separate instrument of the hand.

XXIV.

THE MATTER AND FORM OF ELEMENTARY SUBSTANCES ARE REALLY DISTINCT.

THERE is not much difficulty in proving that between the *materia prima* and the substantial form of an atom there truly is a real distinction. Matter is in its essence passive; while the principle of activity, which the form is, is active. But the relation of the active to the passive is contradictory. Therefore they cannot meet in one being by virtue of one same principle. Hence an atom, being constituted of matter and form, has two principles really distinct from each other.

Secondly, all existing bodies must have density and a determinate figure. The theory of crystallization is founded on that. Now what is the intrinsic cause by which a body, and likewise an atom, has this or that density instead of another? Matter is not the cause of it, being of itself undetermined. Therefore the form is the cause of it. Hence the form is the determining principle, and the matter

MATTER AND FORM OF ELEMENTS. 185

is the determined principle. This necessarily implies a real distinction. St. Thomas remarks that matter without a form could not be constituted into an atom, i.e. into an indivisible substance, in which the parts, though not divided, are really distinct. *Omne corpus divisibile est*, he says. *Omne autem divisibile indiget aliquo continente et uniente partes ejus.* To make this clear, we have only to observe what takes place in plants, in brutes and in man. Whence does their structure, order, and density proceed? Not from matter; for without the vital principle by which it is informed, and from which it is really distinct, *materia prima* is indifferent to every structure, order and density, and when deprived of the vital principle, loses the density, order and figure that it had. Therefore all this proceeds from the same principle that informs the body of the living being. The same reasoning holds good about the forms of the elements in relation to the matter which they inform, viz., that the form and the matter of each element are really distinct.

Thirdly, extension and quantity, like activity and force, are a mode of the elementary atom's being. Now the mode must be in proportion to the modified principle; and therefore the principle of extension is extended, the principle of activity active.

But there is a real distinction between extension and force. Therefore there is a real distinction between the principle of extension, which is matter, and the principle of force, which is form. This is always the way of arguing in philosophy, when treating of acts and of the principles from which they are derived: for, whenever we perceive diversity of acts, we infer diversity of the immediate *potentiæ*, which are their proximate principles.

Here again a comparison will be useful. Suppose that you are pushing some sort of body with your whole hand. In doing so you feel a force that presses and operates on an extended thing, because that which pushes is not a mathematical point, but the whole hand: and hence we deduce with certainty that in the hand there must be, besides the extended matter, a principle of force by which the matter presses that body. Again, when we feel heat, our sensation is evidently a mode of two principles really distinct, from one of which, i.e. the matter, we have extended being, and from the other, i.e. the *anima*, we have the vital affection. In like manner the force manifested by an elementary atom is not in a mathematical point, but in an extended thing: and therefore if the force demonstrates to you a principle of activity, its being in an extended thing shows you the principle of extension really distinct from the principle of activity.

Fourthly, we can find in the natural disposition of simple bodies a proof not without its value. In fact a substance that in its completed essence is simple will certainly not have parts outside of parts. Wherever it is, the whole of it will be; or to use a well-known adage, the whole will be in the whole and in each part. Now this simple substance is *per se* subsistent and therefore *per se* not divisible: but that which is *per se* not divisible cannot be *per se* extended. Therefore a substance that is *per se* simple and subsistent cannot be *per se* extended. So that, unless we deny the real extension of corporeal substances, we must admit that the principles of activity, which the forms are—or as some people call them, forces—receive their being, as extended and divisible things, from another and a different principle, which, being the principle of extension, is matter precisely.

XXV.

AN ELEMENTARY SUBSTANCE IS CHEMICALLY SIMPLE.

I HAVE proved then that an elementary substance is not a simple substance, and is composed of two really distinct principles.

But, though elementary substances are not simple in their essence, they are chemically simple as not being generated by two elementary substances of different natures. All chemists agree in this: that substances obtained by union of substances differing in their nature, are not elementary substances. They are called chemical compounds: and though at one time they were not called so, they were not said to be elementary. But the practical question, "*Which* of them are elementary?" is not a question for philosophers as such to answer. It belongs to the experimental physicists, who by little and little, and after centuries of study, have corrected many errors in purely experimental science.

The proof of this is indisputably evident.

In the corporeal universe there certainly are many substances that differ in their nature specifically, as the specific diversity of their operations plainly shows. These either do or do not result from the union of others. *Non datur medium*, because the opposition is contradictory. If they do not result from the union of substances, they are chemically simple. If they do, we must either admit an endless series of combinations and unions, which is against reason, or come at last to substances chemically simple. In fact the substances that result from the combination of other substances are like numbers, and those that do not like units. However great a number may be, it always consists of units, and proceeds from a unit as from its principle. Thus compound substances are such in relation to their components : and therefore we must acknowledge the components, unless we are prepared to suppose the Begun without a beginning, and the Reasoned without a sufficient reason. But to declare which are simple substances and which are not, belongs to experimental science, and would be foreign to the purpose of a treatise, in which the rational principles only of St. Thomas's Physical system are explained.

Let it suffice for us to infer by reasoning that elementary substances must be of more than one species. I know very well that many scientists would have all elementary substances to be of one specific nature. Why they do so I know not. Perhaps it comes from a natural tendency to suppose in all substances one and the same matter, as the common principle that subjects them to the various transformations on which the unity, order and beauty of the universe depend. But since it is not easy to form a just conception of such matter, those who hardly give a glance at the inmost essence of things may be led to imagine it to be a set of atoms, each having the same nature. Hence the well-known hypotheses of the Epicureans, Cartesians and the modern followers of the Mechanic system. Some few there have been, who, while disowning these theories, and inclining to the Physical system, admitted the double principle of extension and activity, but stood out for the one species of elementary substance, fancying that, as all colours may be had from one light, so may all corporeal substances be constituted from one species of elements. But is that probable?

Most certainly the progress of science has not shown that the elements are of one species. They were at one time reduced by Physicists to a few species: but gradually, as empirical teaching advanced, the species increased, and now there are a great many. This cannot be said to show that the elements are of one species, but contrariwise would lead us infer from experiment what Cardinal Toledo said as a philosopher, viz., that the elements are of more than one species. And in fact, how can they be not of more than one species? The *mixtum* resulting from the elements has a nature different from theirs: but this could not be, if the elements themselves had the same nature. Therefore they differ in nature and consequently in species. If hydrogen and oxygen were the same, the quantity could indeed be increased by aggregation: but not the nature changed belonging thereto.

Anyone seeking to weaken the force of this argument by saying that these, even though of different species, are not chemically simple, because they may be composed of others equal in species, would greatly deceive himself. The proof is of such a sort that its conclusion is universal for chemically simple elements, whatsoever and wheresoever they may be— elements to which we must come in the last resort, unless we like to loiter in the region of the absurd.

There is another objection which at first sight may seem to have some importance: i.e. that a specific diversity in the elements is not required, because an accidental diversity is sufficient. The answer is that it would be sufficient, if the diversity of the *mixta* or compounds were accidental, but not otherwise. Now chemistry shows them to be substantial.

In conclusion, therefore, we say that elementary substances are of different species—are atoms composed of *materia prima* and substantial form—two principles really distinct—and that these elementary substances are simple, being free from chemical composition. This we have defined and proved.

From the elementary we pass on to the mixed or composite.

XXVI.

THE "MIXTUM" OR THE CHEMICAL COMPOUND.
AFFINITY BETWEEN THE ELEMENTS.

IN explaining the Physical system we pointed out that, besides the natural tendency or natural appetite which corporeal substances mutually have, as such, we must admit certain particular tendencies whereby some adhere to others and unite with them, to constitute when united diverse other substances which are called *mixta*, or chemical compounds. These particular tendencies are known by the name of chemical affinities: and we may discuss either their existence or their nature. As to their existence the fact is certain, and so universally admitted, that even those who deny it in theory have to admit it, in fact, at every step, when they mean to discourse, and not talk nonsense, about the changes of corporeal substances. We shall not waste words about that, but say something about their natures.

And here it is well to remember what was said before about mechanical motion, which is forced, because extrinsically produced, and therefore has no natural direction or term fixed at which the motion would cease. No one will deny the fact that every corporeal substance may be subjected to mechanical impulses, and then moved *ab extrinseco:* but to suppose that chemical affinities originate from them would be utterly unreasonable and not worth a serious argument. God willed that in corporeal nature there should be a various and continual succession, in which, as St. Augustine says, "the morning of things always comes after the evening." Therefore He gave to the elementary substances that active principle by which they are constituted in their specific being, and from which those particular tendencies follow that go by the name of affinities. Moreover, as if to assure us of the fact that even beings without knowledge have these particular tendencies, He willed that in beings there should be a gradual descent from the most perfect animal down to inorganic substance, not only without knowledge but also without life. Common sense tells us that the movement of a horse or of a lion to a certain spot is by an inner principle of nature: but when, in the order of sensitive beings, we come to the lowest species, such as zoophytes, many people find it hard to see how certain motions can be accounted for on the same principle.

Nevertheless analogy alone ought to persuade us of the fact, and make us listen to the suggestions of reason, instead of being carried away by the allurements of imagination. But if this applies to zoophytes, it also applies to inorganic substances tending towards a certain determinate end: so that sound reasoning rejects the mere external principles of mechanical motion as quite improbable. If it be absurd, as in fact it is, to say that a stone pitched at a man is attracted by the man hit, equally absurd is it to assert, as some chemists do, that the elementary atoms are moved and directed to unite by external impulses, and yet have a mutual affinity.

We must remark that chemical affinities take place between those substances only which, when afterwards combined, give, as the result of the combination, another substance, whose nature differs from theirs. And since, as we have said, the components also must therefore be of diverse natures, chemical affinities therefore cannot take place otherwise than between elementary substances differing from each other.

This affinity may be subject to accidental modifications: for if plants, brutes, men and angels are subject to accidental changes while retaining their own nature, how can we except elementary atoms, placed in the lowest grade of being? The Physical system says that we cannot. Reason and experience give the same answer. For in an elementary atom there is extension and the principle of activity or force: and the former can undergo changes in the more or less, while the latter can be altered by contrary force. Thus we can see clearly that elements operate under some circumstances, and under others do not, or that, if they do, their operation is weak, though not specifically different. No wonder then if the different states, if the different modifications to which the atoms are subject, either impede or promote the appearance of chemical affinities: for this is quite natural, as we may judge by the analogy between the proper tendencies of living beings and the affinities of things without life. Hence the common saying of chemists that affinity varies very much, according to the various dispositions in which bodies are found. In fact the elements that have affinity to each other cannot combine otherwise than by mutual operation, to which they either are, or are not disposed in themselves. If they are so, proximity and contact will suffice to set going their reciprocal action. If not, they must be disposed from without. Hence the necessity of an extrinsic agent, to operate on them and alter them, as heat and electricity are known to do. Some, it is true, have asserted that the mere presence of some determinate substance is sufficient to make the elements operate: but if this is to be understood strictly, so as not to imply true action, it is trifling and false. What is it present for, if it does nothing? To introduce that in chemical combinations for the purpose of awakening affinity, is out of the question, and multiplies beings without necessity, against the well known axiom, *Entia non sunt multiplicanda sine necessitate.*

And let this be sufficient about affinity, according to the principles of the Physical system: for we have shown that system to be in conformity with science and explanatory of the facts that science undertakes to investigate therein.

XXVII.

THE "MIXTUM," OR CHEMICAL COMPOUND, HAS A NATURE SPECIFICALLY DIFFERENT FROM THAT OF ITS COMPONENTS.

A SUBSTANCE that proceeds from the coupling together or combination of elements is called a *mixtum*, or more commonly a chemical compound. Such for instance is cuniaber, or water—the one resulting from sulphur and quicksilver, the other from hydrogen and oxygen. The species of the elements of corporeal substances are very few in number, when compared with those of the *mixta* derived from them, as the letters of the alphabet are very few in comparison with the innumerable words which they compose. We willingly acknowledge that in these days, by means of diligent and repeated experiments, wonderful discoveries have been made about the manifold formation of the *mixta:* but their essence is passed over very lightly, though deserving particular study.

The *mixtum* or true chemical compound has

a nature specifically different from that of each element of which it is composed; and when this is not verified, the elements cannot be chemically combined, nor can the body resulting from the combination be a *mixtum*, but may be called an aggregate or a mingled mass. The specific diversity is manifested to us by the constant diversity of their operation, because *operari sequitur esse:* and this is the only but certain means by which we are able to infer the diversity of the active principle that informs them.

Suppose, for instance, that into an empty vase of glass with the metallic wire in it you introduce oxygen and hydrogen in proportion of volume as one to two, and by the help of the metallic wire strike out the electric spark. There is an instantaneous combustion. The fluids disappear, and little drops of water appear, occupying a space two thousand times less than what was occupied by the oxygen and hydrogen. Now let us consider the mutual relations of these elements to each other and to the water generated from them.

The specific weight of the oxygen is eight times that of the hydrogen at the same temperature. Oxygen will burn, hydrogen will not. Animals inhale oxygen, and not hydrogen. All the specific properties of the one are different from those of the other: and though they have generic properties in common, such as that of being extended, heavy, resistent, the one has positive while the other has negative electricity, and their capacity of heat differs. Their diversity of nature, therefore, could not be more evident. And yet that spark makes all these differences disappear. Instead of the fluids there is one liquid—water, whose properties have nothing to do with the vanished elements. The specific weight is different and so is the capacity of heat. Though generated from oxygen as much as from hydrogen, it extinguishes fire instead of feeding it. Formed from oxygen and hydrogen, its operation in inorganic things differs widely from theirs, and is different again in plants, in brutes, in man : so that in the operation of water we no more recognize that of oxygen and hydrogen than we recognize the operation of clay in that of gold or silver. Evidently therefore the nature of water differs from that of oxygen and of hydrogen just as the nature of clay differs from the nature of gold or of silver : and therefore the nature of water is specifically different from the nature of the oxygen and of the hydrogen from which it was generated. This holds good of every true *mixtum*, or chemical compound, in relation to its components.

XXVIII.

WHAT IS MEANT BY SUBSTANTIAL TRANSFORMATION.

SOME people seem to think that substantial transformation, as understood according to the Physical system, means annihilation of the elements, or at least of their substantial forms, and the production of a new form to be the specific principle of the chemical compound's activity. If so, we should not have a chemical composition, but annihilation and creation. *Mixtio*, says Aristotle, *est alteratorum unio.** It therefore consists in this: When, e.g. oxygen and hydrogen combine, there remains, 1°. the matter *(materia prima)* of both; 2°. in each the principle of activity undergoes a change; 3°. by virtue of this change every atomic part of the compound molecule has in itself the nature of the *mixtum;* so that every atomic part of the water has the nature of water, and the qualities of the previous elements (oxygen

---
* *De Gener.,* i.

and hydrogen) are hidden. All this implies a substantial transformation of the elements. That, in virtue of this, the *mixtum* is a whole, of a new and homogeneous nature in every part, is taught by Aristotle. He says: "Is a *mixtum* nothing else than minute particles varying in their nature, but so confused that, although retaining their former nature, they seem a homogeneous whole? No: for in the *mixtum* every part must have the nature of the whole, as each part of water has the nature of water." This principle of his is quite in accordance with the division of elements into atoms and the disposal of the *mixtum* into molecules of a certain dimension and a certain figure.

People are so afraid of this in our times, that a few words about it may not be amiss. We said before that every substantial form requires determinate matter, and must naturally have also, according to its various states, a determinate figure. *Oportet ut determinatæ formæ determinata figura debeatur.** In that which has life the substantial form requires a determinate organism: and thus the soul, which is the substantial form of the human body, could not be adapted to the organism of an eagle, nor the substantial form of a stag to that of a fish, nor the substantial form of a peach-

---

* *Comm. in Sent.*, ii. Dist. xix. 1, 1.

tree to that of a camellia or of a tulip. Now this doctrine must be equally true of the inorganic : so that, in virtue of a substantial form, an atom of gold has not under the same temperature the same figure as an atom of phosphorus, nor has a molecule of a mixed body the same figure as that of another mixed body. True it is that there are bodies, both elementary and mixed, whose atoms or molecules, in a solid state, show equal figures, and therefore may be called isomorphous : but that is not in contradiction with the doctrine. Rather does it lead thereto by a sort of analogy ; for in the different species the likeness between the external form or figures of bodies becomes greater as the species descend from Man, the noblest of the animates, towards the lowest species of corporeal substances. Anyone may see that what we have said about the atoms of the simple bodies and the molecules of the mixed is in no way against those beautiful theories about crystals, which are so deservedly honoured in physics.

XXIX.

THE COMMON SENSE OF MANKIND IS IN FAVOUR OF A BELIEF IN THE TRUE SUBSTANTIAL TRANSFORMATION OF THE ELEMENTS.

THAT in mixed or composite bodies the transformation produces another nature totally different from the nature of its components, is so evident to the senses that it has no need of further proof. Hence it is a universal and rooted belief. A man of plain common sense would laugh if you said to him, " You must know that which you suppose to be water is nothing of the sort, but only what two other substances, quite different, seem to be, just as a circular piece of wood with seven colours painted on it seems white, if you turn it round very fast." Nature tells us the contrary, and language, that faithfully interprets the common sentiments of mankind, confirms the same truth. It has always been said, and is said by learned and ignorant, that the chemical compound has a new nature, a nature different from that of its elements.

The chemists also say the same, even those who deny it theoretically and think that in the *mixtum* or compound the elements remain just as they were before the combination. Moreover, the words "unity of nature" mean unity of the active principle, not a co-operation of different operators for one and the same end.

To this common language St. Thomas appealed when showing, against Eutyches, that in Christ there cannot be one nature only, because the divine and the human nature are permanent in Him. A *one* results from many, he says, firstly in virtue of order only, as one city is composed of many houses, and one army out of many soldiers. Secondly, in virtue of order and composition; as one house is made of many parts by mutual contact and joining. But these ways, he says, "will not suffice to make one nature from many: and therefore those things whose form is only order and composition are not natural in such a way that their unity may be called unity of nature." He goes on to say: "Never is it found that one nature comes to be, out of two natures remaining such, because each nature is a whole, and those things out of which anything is constituted have the relation of parts. Wherefore, since the result of the soul's union with the body is one individual, neither the body nor the soul can be said to be a nature in the sense in which we are now using the word, because neither the one nor the other has a complete species, but each is a part of one nature. Therefore, since human nature and the Divine Nature are each a complete nature, it is impossible for them to concur in making one nature, without one or both ceasing to be: which is not possible, because it is evident from what has been said that one Christ is true God and true man. It is therefore impossible that in Christ there can be one nature only."*

Here we can see incidentally what mischief may be done by an easy twisting of words from the sense in which they are commonly understood, for the purpose of furthering particular opinions. Those therefore who will not allow that the nature of the elements is changed in the *mixtum* or compound, should call the compound an aggregate or a mingling together or anything they please, but not a new nature; or they will not only come into collision with words that are used and must be used in Theology, but also be at variance with the common language of mankind.

---

* *Contra Gent.*, iv. 35.

XXX.

THE SUBSTANTIAL TRANSFORMATION OF THE ELEMENTS IS PROVED BY FACTS.

IN fact the mixtum or chemical compound is a substance that has properties and operations invariably different from those of the elements of which it is composed: but the principle of activity, or substantial form, is the source of the properties and of the operations. Therefore the substantial form of the elements, which is really distinct from their matter, is different from the substantial form of the *mixtum*; and so, in that passing from the state of being elements to the state of being a chemical compound, there was a true substantial change. Now what is there to be said against this argument? Can the elements co-operate to the same term of operations, and thus operate in specifically different ways, retaining their own proper principles as before? This cannot be. The operations resulting from co-operation of separate principles must reveal the disposition of these principles, either in an equal degree, or as shewing what more belongs to the stronger. Thus, for instance, if the two elements disjoined attract a substance, together they will attract it more strongly: and if one of them attracts while the other repels, the attraction and repulsion will be according to the difference of their contrary forces. Can it be said that the elements themselves by virtue of their union, not only co-operate to a term of operation, but give besides one sole principle of it? This would suppose the impossibility, that each atom remains in the *mixtum* as a true individual in its own nature. St. Thomas therefore says:

"It is impossible that of things different in being there should be one operation. I say 'one,' not speaking of the term, but of its proceeding from the operator. For many men pulling a ship do one action as to the thing operated on, which is one: but on the part of the pullers there are many operations, because there are diverse impulses moving it." *

Moreover, all that under the opposite hypotheses is inexplicable, has, at least, a satisfactory explanation in the thesis that we are defending: and therefore for that reason alone,

---

* *Contra Gent.*, ii. 57.

if there were no other, it ought to be preferred. In fact, if anyone asks why in chemical combination there is often a species of agitation or conflict or confusion between the combining substances, while everything goes peacefully, so to speak, in perfect crystallization, the reason is this: In chemical combination, the elements operate on each other with a force that ever changes their principle of activity. In crystallization the atoms or molecules have only to dispose themselves conformably with their angles and facets in a determinate, symmetrical order; to which accurate disposition of parts the impetus and violence often noticed in chemical combination would be hurtful. And if it be asked why a crystal may have its forms totally ruined by mechanical means, whilst a *mixtum* or compound never can be decomposed in that way, the answer is evident in the fact that in a crystal the atoms or molecules are suitably disposed, but not transformed. A merely mechanical cause, therefore, suffices to break them apart and spoil their symmetry; whereas in a *mixtum* or compound the elements are not only disposed in a certain manner, but also have their nature changed. To re-establish these in their former substantial being requires a cause contrary in effectiveness to that which transformed them. So can heat decompose a *mixtum* or compound, when it has force enough to take away in the principles of activity the change that happened at the moment of combination. So can another element do, with the concurrence of heat, and combine with an element that was with another or with others in the *mixtum*. In this way we can give a suitable reason for the facts: but to say that electricity, heat and other causes, which extrinsically concur in chemical combinations, can only shove atoms and make them group themselves by twos and threes, giving place to some and resisting others, is inexplicable and against experience.

XXXI.

CONCERNING THE OPPOSITION TO THE DOCTRINE OF SUBSTANTIAL TRANSFORMATION.

IN science as in politics innovation is now the rule. The supporters of error do their utmost to hide away by means of silence the demonstrations of truth, which would contradict their theories, endeavouring to make the friends of truth contemptible and odious by attributing to them strange and absurd doctrines which they never dreamt of advocating. So it is in the present controversy. According to our opponents the philosophy of St. Thomas is against the progress of physical science, and his modern disciples are supposed either to ignore or deny facts that are certain in modern chemistry. But will they be so good as to tell us what these facts are?

We say that a substantial transformation of the components in a *mixtum*, i.e. in a chemical compound, requires the components to be of different natures, with affinity to each other, as before stated. But this is an assured fact, and generally accepted as such by the chemists themselves. We say moreover that the elementary substances which compose the *mixtum* must be in truly physical contact, and if chemists forget to affirm this, reason will remind them. For, if the elements remained at a distance from each other, they could not possibly form one compound substance, and therefore could not operate as such. If the distance between them, however small, were absolute, they could not operate on each other at all, because, as we have clearly shewn, *actio in distans repugnat.*

Since then they must come into contact, their dimensions must be of the smallest. Hence the well known axiom : *Corpora non agunt nisi soluta.* For if there sometimes is a chemical combination between bodies that are not so small, then that chemical combination is on the surface; as when, for instance, a thick bar of iron is by exposure to damp gradually changed into rust, i.e. hydrate of sesqui-oxide of iron.

In reply we are told that, according to the chemists, the elementary substances, besides differing in nature, are reduced to the condition of atoms, which have a determinate volume and weight and are placed in a certain position relatively to each other. But we have nothing to say against that. Why should we, when it agrees quite well with the principles of St. Thomas? But the elements, they say, must be atoms in order to combine chemically. Very well, but we have a clear and precise conception of an atom, and the modern writers on chemistry have not. What do they mean by an atom? According to its etymology it means that which, whatever its size may be, is not divided, and therefore among the Greeks we find the word used of a beard, or of grass, to signify being uncut. But if you take it to mean a very small substance, you will find that in modern use the smallness is arbitrary and indeterminate. Moreover in the division of bodies modern writers consider the quantity alone: and we clearly shewed,* when treating of the divisibility of bodies, that, so considered, all bodies must be conceived as divisible *ad infinitum*. A true atom is indivisible, being the minimum in its own nature. It cannot, remaining what it is, be divided any more. The modern men cannot give any reason for this: but St. Thomas has taught us that quantity is an accident of bodies, and that if you divide a body till the substance can no longer produce this accident, the substance, no longer having quantity, will be indivisible. We, having

---
* Chapter XX.

already explained this doctrine of the Angelic Doctor, can say, in accordance with his principles, that every species of elementary substance has its atoms, each of which must be a *minimum:* so that we have no difficulty about admitting elementary atoms in the generation of *mixta,* i.e. chemical compounds.

Consequently, we can admit without any difficulty that the number of these atoms or elementary *minima* is by nature determined for making this or that combination, from which one or another compound substance is generated. If they say that it requires two atoms of x and one of y to make the compound substance a, we have nothing to object. If they tell us that with the variation of numerical proportions the substances will vary, so be it, provided that the assertion be justified by fact.

Clearly these elements, though they are atoms or *minima,* i.e. reduced to the smallest possible quantity, are extended, are true bodies, are subject to universal attraction, have a determinate weight. Therefore we can admit the theory respecting the atomic weight of the aforesaid elements.

Also, by reason of their being truly extended bodies, they must unite not only in determinate atomic weight, but in determinate proportional volumes.

If these elementary *minima* occupy space, as they certainly do, each of them will be in a certain position with respect to the others. Therefore, when certain chemists propose certain symbolical figures, to indicate the place where, in order that the chemical combination may take place, the elementary atoms have to be, we do not say that such figures are in themselves absurd, though they cannot be proved by experiments.

Now, seeing that we accept these theories and all the chemical laws founded on facts, by what right can we be accused of being in opposition to chemistry and the progress of science?

But the adversaries of St. Thomas and of his followers put forward a most important point of disagreement, on which modern chemistry quite condemns the physics of the Angelic Doctor. I allude to the substantial transformation of the *mixtum* or chemical compound, generated from elements.

To penetrate the meaning of St. Thomas, we must think philosophically: but the empirical mind is offended at being required to do that, and follows the easy teaching of Epicurus, which amounts to this: That the world is an innumerable quantity of atoms, gifted somehow with extension and capable of knocking against other atoms, or of being knocked against by them. The only difference between these atoms is that some are smooth, some pointed: yet their agglomeration in a certain number gives us all the different substances that are. This is quite clear, but certainly not reasonable: and Cicero, following the principles of Plato and of Aristotle, ridicules it in the person of a certain Amafanius. *Tam vero physica,* he says, *si Epicurum et Democritum probarem, possem scribere ita plane ut Amafanius* (in company with the modern Epicureans, who make all inorganic things and all living things, including men, come out of atomic aggregations.) *Quid est enim magnum, quum causas rerum efficientes sustuleris, de corpusculorum, ita enim appellant atomos, concussione fortuita loqui? Nostra tu physica nosti, quæ continentur ex effectione et ex materia ea quam format et fingit effectio.* (*Acad.*, ii.) In these last words the Physical system of matter and form is clearly meant. Moreover he says further on: *De natura rerum ita dicebant* (Plato and Aristotle), *ut eam dividerent in res duas, ut altera esset efficiens* (in other words, the form:) *altera quasi huic se præbens* (i.e. the matter), *ea quæ efficeretur aliquid. In eo quod efficeret, vim esse censebant; in eo autem quod efficeretur, materiam quamdam; in utroque tamen utrumque. Neque enim materia ipsa coalescere potuisset, si nulla vi contineretur, neque vis sine aliqua materia. Nihil est enim quod alicubi esse cogatur. Sed quod* EX UTROQUE *id jam corpus nominabant. (Acad.,* vi.) Here he clearly acknowledges the fact that all bodies are constituted of two principles really distinct, viz., matter and form. Anyone who can read Latin and understand the meaning of words must see that. The conclusion is that, like Cicero, we must reckon this Epicurean chemistry among the chatterings of quacks, as also the Darwinian system, which is founded on it.

When we affirm the fact that a true chemical compound is a body generated by the chemical combination of elements differing from each other in their nature and that the body generated therefrom differs from its elements, do we not say what is said *expressis terminis* by every modern chemist, seeing that all of them find therein precisely the difference between chemical compounds and mere mingling of things? Moreover we express an incontrovertible fact, inasmuch as the nature of a body is the principle of operation that determines its species.

"True," they say, "elements of different natures are required for the generation of a chemical compound: but chemical compounds decompose into their own elements. This upsets your formula that compounds differ in nature from their elementary compounds."

Yes, we do say that the elements are of different natures, and that the *mixtum* or chemical compound decomposes into its elements—e.g. that water when decomposed becomes oxygen and hydrogen, that in the water there is no trace of the elements oxygen and hydrogen. Therefore we have to say that in the water the oxygen and hydrogen exist, but not as such. But then, how *do* they exist?

There are three ways in which a thing may exist in another thing : viz., *formaliter, in potentia, virtualiter*. It exists in another thing formally *(formaliter)*, when it exists there in its own form. The likeness of St. Thomas, for instance, exists formally in the block of marble out of which it was sculptured, and a chicken exists formally within the shell of a fertilized egg after incubation. If that block of marble has not yet been sculptured, the likeness is only *in potentia*, because the artist may sculpture it into the likeness of St. Thomas or of any one else ; and if the egg were not fertilized, the chicken would remain *in potentia*. A thing exists in another *in virtute*, when it is there neither formally nor merely *in potentia*, but has in itself an inner virtue by which it, and nothing else, can or should proceed therefrom; as, for instance, in a fertilized egg there is an inward virtue by which, given the requisite conditions, a chicken is formed of the same species as that whence the seminal virtue was derived.

We say then, first of all, that the elements of a chemical body are not formally in it, because if they were so, the chemical body would be nothing more than an aggregate of different substances; which is contradicted by fact. Secondly, we say that they are not there merely *in potentia*, because the said chemical body cannot decompose into any other elements. It follows then that the elements are in the *mixtum in virtute*, because the *mixtum* has an inward disposition to decompose, under certain circumstances, into those elements, and not into any others.

Therefore they who accuse us of believing that a *mixtum* cannot be generated without the annihilation of its elements, or that nothing but *materia prima* remains in it, speak ignorantly, because the re-appearance of the elements by resolution of the *mixtum* clearly shews that somehow they had remained. The illustrious Cardinal Toledo (Lib. II. *De Gen. et Corr.*) deduces the existence of the elements precisely from the fact that the *mixtum* is resolved into them. *Patet*, he says, *quod quæ resolvuntur componuntur ex illis in quæ resolvuntur. Quumque in resolutionibus non sit processus infinitus, oportet fateri esse corpora non resolubilia in alia corpora. Talia igitur erunt elementa.* Not only must the compound be capable of resolving into its elements, but the elements must be found in the *mixtum*, for at Chap. I. he says, TRES CONDITIONES DEBERE INESSE ELEMENTO. PRIMA *ut ex eo aliquid fiat... Secunda, ut insit in re quæ fit. ... Tertia, ut sit primum ex quo fit res, et ultimum in quod dividitur. Adverte autem, quod debet esse elementum simplex, id est non resolubile in partes differentes specie: non enim repugnat elemento dividi in partes quantitatis, ut literæ elementa sunt dictionum, et partes habent literæ ipsæ.*

Certain it is then that the elements do exist in the *mixtum*, and equally certain that things exist in it, as we have said, neither *formaliter*, nor merely *in potentia*, but *in virtute*. That they are virtually there is proved by the fact that something within disposes the compound for decomposing into the elements from which it was generated, and not into any others. *Formæ elementorum*, says St. Thomas,[*] *manent in mixto non actu, sed virtute: manent enim qualitates propriæ elementorum, licet remissæ, in quibus est virtus formarum*

---
[*] *Summa*, P. i. Q. lxxvi. a. 4 ad 4.

elementarium. Et hujusmodi qualitas mixtionis est propria dispositio ad formam substantialem corporis mixti; puta formam lapidis, vel animati cujuscumque.

Thus does the Angelic Doctor shew that the nature of the component elements is changed into the nature of the *mixtum*: but let us go a little further into his meaning.

What is meant by the *substantial form* of the elements and of the *mixtum?* The substantial form is the active principle that specificates a material being [*esse*], and it differs in the different beings [*entia*] that have different natures. This substantial form, specificating the being [*ens*], is not immutable, but can be changed by a proportionate external agent. When the specificating principle has changed, the being [*ens*] cannot remain unchanged: and therefore when the substantial form of the elements is specifically changed, so as to become the form of a *mixtum*, changed must the elements be into the nature of that *mixtum*.

These substantial forms are not subsistent forces, neither are they made identical with the matter which they inform: but each of them, with the matter which it informs, constitutes one *ens*.

Each *ens* (as we have shewn when speaking of qualities) has certain qualities, generic or specific, rooted in its substantial form. Therefore every element has its qualities, according to the nature of its substantial form, and every *mixtum* has its qualities according to its form.

Now the internal disposition of a subject to be actuated through extrinsic action by one form, rather than by another, is reducible to the genus of quality. *Quidquid recipitur*, says an old and wise adage, *per modum recipientis recipitur;* and hence an external agent operating on an *ens* will, as to its form, produce a change in proportion to its qualities. But when one *ens* changes into another, the qualities that preceded the change are *not* isolated and without a foundation in any substantial form. The new form beginning becomes the foundation of those qualities that were in the preceding form; and the preceding form ceases to be when the new form begins, because it is not conceivable that, even for a moment, there should be neither the old form nor the new—no form at all. As the weight of a waggon presses continually on its wheels, and is never without a fulcrum, though the spokes are moving in succession, so do the qualities of an *ens* continue to exist in a succession of different substantial forms: and the fact is clearly shown in the generation and corruption of inorganic bodies, of plants, of animals, and even of man. Rightly then was it said that the qualities of the elements are the disposition to the form of the *mixtum* or compound, and that such qualities remain after the generation of the *mixtum*: and therefore that they are the inner cause by which, under the action of a cause that destroys the substantial form of the *mixtum*, the elements of which it was constituted reappear. But these qualities cannot reappear with their primal energy; for they are no longer the elements in their own natures, but qualities relaxed or neutralized.

Synthetically then, we say this: 1°. The concurrence of various elements in the generation of a chemical compound is undeniable. 2°. Undeniable is it that in the compound there exists a principle of activity different from that which was in each element. 3°. It is a fact that, by reason of this change of the principle of activity, the nature and substance of the *mixtum* are different from the nature and substance of the elements, and are said to be so by the chemists, who therein precisely find the difference between a chemical combination and a mere mingling of different things. Let us accept these facts then as reasonable, and endeavour to explain reasonably the phenomenon of substantial change in the elements, however difficult it may be.

Certain men, however, wishing to follow the variable opinion of so-called scientists, admit the facts, yet with a strange incoherence deny the substantial change, because they cannot explain it, though, as we have seen, it is essentially connected with those facts. "Had it been known," says a modern writer, "that we can obtain safe and sound from the new body, by chemical analysis, the two or more substances in whose combination it originated," (here he cooly ignores the fact that the Scholastics did know it), "they would have said, as we say now, that it is not easy to explain how and why the intimate union of two substances gives to the total thereby produced qualities so very different from those of the component substances; but that does not confer on us the right to suppose a change of nature and essence in those substances."

This is nonsense. He might indeed tell us that the fact is difficult to explain, but it is irrational to contradict oneself by affirming a fact and then denying it in other words.

Some will say that we are insisting too stiffly on the importance of substantial changes. But, indeed, the question is of the greatest moment. It is disgraceful to profess error in science, especially when it opens the door to errors universal and most pernicious. He who errs about the essence must err about the powers and operations, because the powers and operations of things are derived from their essence.

By reason of having denied that the essence of bodies is composed of matter and form, a considerable number among the cultivators of the physical sciences rushed into atomism and evolutionism and that monistic theory which is downright materialism, in which they are already admitting that all is matter and motion, from which, after accepting the famous principle of "stored motion" in organic and inorganic things, they fall so low as to agree with the physicist Voght, that thoughts are to the brain as the bile is to the liver. "In that struggle of the spirit which is now going on," says Hæckel, in his autobiography, "the war-trumpet announces the dawn of a new day that will end the conflicts of the middle ages. In the war, undertaken in the name of truth" (which is extinguished now in almost all the universities), "the theory of evolution takes the part of heavy artillery. Before the heavy blows of this monistic artillery the tents of the dualistic sophisms (i.e. soul and body, form and matter) tumble down. The proud edifice of the hierarchy and the rock of the Infallibility-dogma shake and fall like houses of cards. All the libraries of ecclesiastical science and retrograde philosophy vanish before the enlightening theory of evolution.* Bois-Raymond, denying the composition of matter and form, body and soul, discourses in the following fashion: "Suppose that all the atoms which constituted Cæsar were by mechanical art put in their proper places (this, according to atomists would be a substantial composition) and that on them were impressed their velocity and their direction. We say that Cæsar would then reappear in body and soul. The artificial Cæsar would at once have the same sensations, the same desires, the same thoughts that its model had when he stood by the Rubicon. Its memory would be full of the same images. It would have the same faculties, inherited and acquired. Suppose that, at the same instant, the same *mechanical* work were done in several places by the same atoms of carbon, hydrogen, &c., how could so many Cæsars be distinguished from each other except by reason of the place in which they were made and equalized?" †

The professor and senator Moleschott, who is now ‡ grieving over the deaths of his wife and daughter, does not call this hypothesis absurd, nor does he object to the theory of

---
* This inflated abuse of matter and form will serve to shew what he, *et hoc genus omne*, think about the importance of the doctrine. *Verbum sapienti.*

† *Les Bornes de la Philosophie Naturelle.*

‡ I.e., when Father Cornoldi was writing this chapter.—*Trans.*

thus making up an animated Cæsar, but he cannot see his way to find the means of doing so. Such are the illustrious men who now fill our professorial chairs. If such principles were universally admitted, there would of course be no religion; for there would be no reason, and without reason religion is impossible. Such are the weapons used by these teachers against the Holy See, against the Church, against religion, against God. They put nonsense in the place of truth, and then say that religion and faith are irreconcilable with science. Who can fail to see that these questions are of the greatest moment? On them depends, not merely the progress of science, but even its very existence.

In this treatise on the Physical system of St. Thomas we have explained those doctrines only of the Angelic Doctor that were less known, most important and that closely concern biology and anthropology, on which we had enlarged before. We might have touched upon a fundamental point respecting the distinction between essence and existence: but inasmuch as this requires to be discussed well—has difficulties in it more than a few, chiefly owing to the cavils of objectors, and has been sufficiently explained by us in the *Civiltà Cattolica* (Serie xii. Vol. vi. p. 305), we refer the reader thereto. And so we stop here, hoping that what we have written will serve, not only to remove many inveterate prejudices against the ill-known Scholastic doctrine, but also to make scientists pause on the edge of the abyss and reconsider their teaching, which indeed is so bad that the errors taught in former times are comparatively unimportant.

THE END.

www.ingramcontent.com/pod-product-compliance
Lightning Source LLC
Chambersburg PA
CBHW031743230426
43669CB00007B/458